LEARNING 1ST GRADE MATH WORKBOOK

1st grade math activity book with money, telling time, and addition and subtraction practice to prepare your child for 2nd grade

Autumn McKay

> Find me on Instagram!
> @BestMomIdeas

Learning 1ˢᵗ Grade Math Workbook by Autumn McKay
Published by Creative Ideas Publishing

www.BestMomIdeas.com

© 2020 Autumn McKay

All rights reserved. No portion of this book may be reproduced in any form without permission from the author, except as permitted by U.S. copyright law.

For permissions contact:
Permissions@BestMomIdeas.com

ISBN: 978-1-952016-26-4

Table of Contents

Place Value 1
Addition 12
Subtraction 26
Money 40
Time 54
Fractions 66
Measurements 77
Word Problems 100

Introduction

I'm going to use the pronoun he throughout the introduction, but please know I thought of your sweet little girl too as I created this book.

I'm so glad to be a part of your 1st grader's journey to learn math to help prepare him for 2nd grade! It is my hope that you and your child have fun as he learns basic math skills. In this book you will find many activity pages to help your 1st grader master math concepts in an exciting way.

Early math exposure is a strong predictor for future success, not only in math, but also in reading and critical thinking skills. When a child is exposed to math early he is able to communicate more effectively using mathematics. For example, "I want 5 purple stickers" opposed to, "I want stickers." Learning math helps deepen an understanding of math concepts, vocabulary, and critical thinking skills. All of these skills help to develop a mentally organized way of thinking which can lead to better comprehension for reading—a child is able to organize the parts of a story to better understand it.

Here are a few tips and suggestions I recommend for using this book:

- First and foremost, have fun with your child as he is learning these math skills! The objective of this book is to help your child learn math, but also to build his confidence as he is learning new information.

- Sit with your child as he is working through the workbook. Read the directions together, offer guidance when needed, and be there to answer questions as they may arise.

- You are welcome to choose the order in which you would like to complete the book, but I do recommend focusing on one concept at a time.

- As you and your child are learning new math skills be sure to practice using them in the real world too. Ask him to count out the cash for receipts, ask him for the time, cook together, and solve problems together. This will help him to become more familiar with the new math skills he is learning.

- Feel free to contact me if you have any questions or concerns at Autumn@BestMomIdeas.com.

Most importantly, let your child have fun and enjoy the learning process!

PLACE VALUE

TENS AND ONES

Count the tens and ones in each box. Write the answer in the appropriate box.

tens	ones
1	1

tens	ones
3	5

tens	ones
5	6

tens	ones
2	7

tens	ones
8	2

tens	ones
5	7

COLOR TENS AND ONES

Color the correct tens and ones to show each written number.

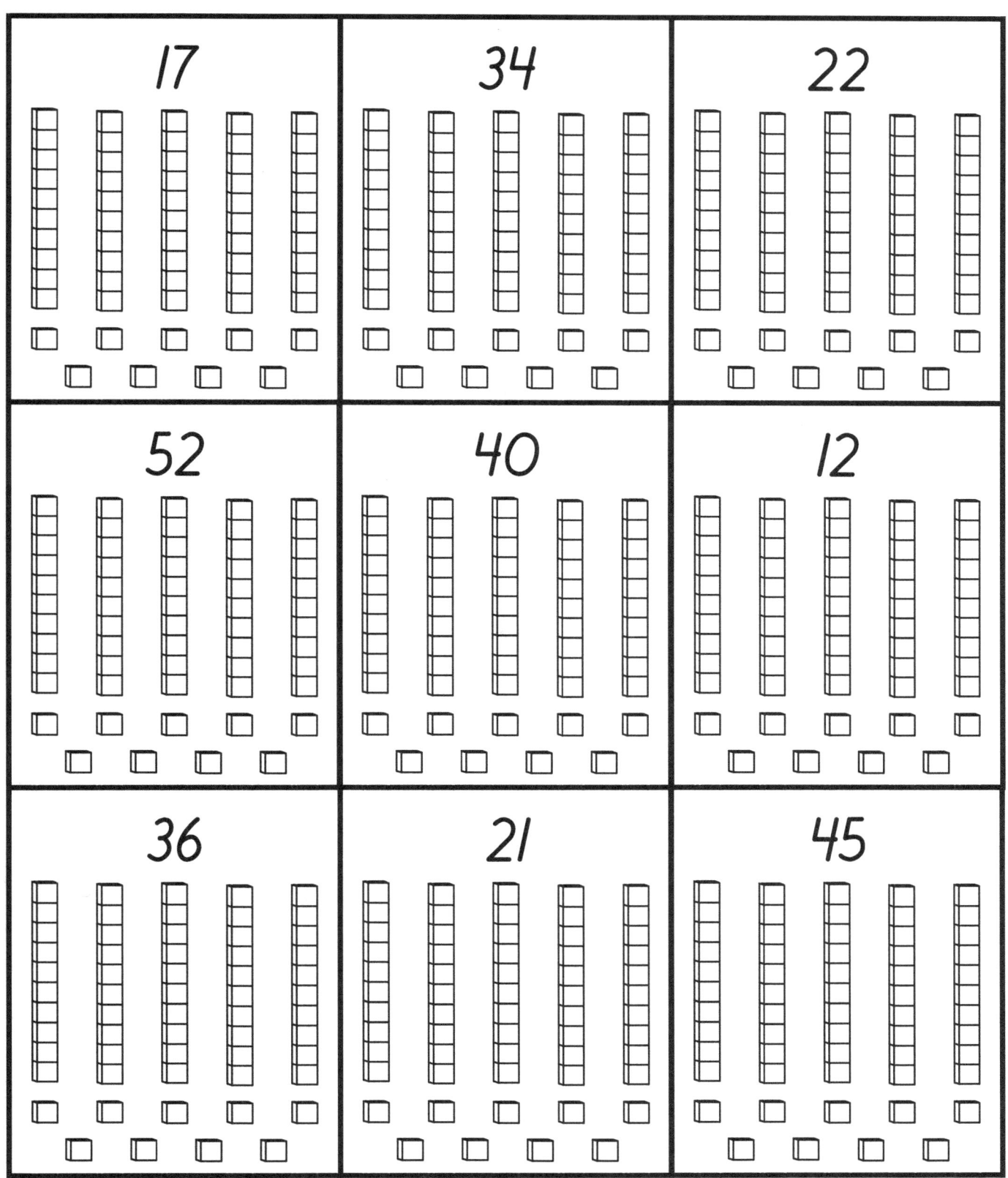

TENS AND ONES 2

Fill in the tens and ones blanks. Then complete the math problem.

_2_ tens _8_ ones _20_ + _8_ = _28_	___ tens ___ ones ___ + ___ = ___
___ tens ___ ones ___ + ___ = ___	___ tens ___ ones ___ + ___ = ___
___ tens ___ ones ___ + ___ = ___	___ tens ___ ones ___ + ___ = ___

DRAW TENS AND ONES

Draw sticks and dots to represent the number shown.

Tens	Ones
|	• • •

13

Tens	Ones

18

Tens	Ones

11

Tens	Ones

41

Tens	Ones

38

Tens	Ones

16

Tens	Ones

20

Tens	Ones

55

Tens	Ones

12

PLACE VALUE

Find the answer for each problem.

___ tens ___ ones ___	___ tens ___ ones ___	___ tens ___ ones ___
___ tens ___ ones ___	___ tens ___ ones ___	___ tens ___ ones ___
___ tens ___ ones ___	___ tens ___ ones ___	___ tens ___ ones ___
___ tens ___ ones ___	___ tens ___ ones ___	___ tens ___ ones ___

WHAT'S THE NUMBER?

Read the clue. Draw the answer. Write the numerical answer.

Clue	Draw it	Write it	Clue	Draw it	Write it
Two tens and six ones.			Four tens and four ones.		
Two tens and eight ones.			One ten and two ones.		
Three tens and five ones.			Five tens and three ones.		
Two tens and four ones.			One ten and five ones.		
One ten and eight ones.			Four tens and zero ones.		

COMPARING NUMBERS

Write how many tens and ones are on each side. Compare the numbers. Write greater than (>), less than (<), or equal (=).

HOW MANY BLOCKS?

The big blocks respresent 100 blocks. Write down how many blocks are in each set.

100 100 [tens] [one]	100 [tens] [ones]
_____ blocks	_____ blocks
100 100 [tens] [ones]	100 100 100 [ones]
_____ blocks	_____ blocks
100 [tens] [ones]	100 100 [tens] [ones]
_____ blocks	_____ blocks
100 100 100 / 100 100 [tens] [ones]	100 100 100 / 100 [tens] [ones]
_____ blocks	_____ blocks

Learning 1st Grade Math Workbook | Autumn McKay

COLOR THE BLOCKS

Color the correct hundreds, tens, and ones to represent each number shown.

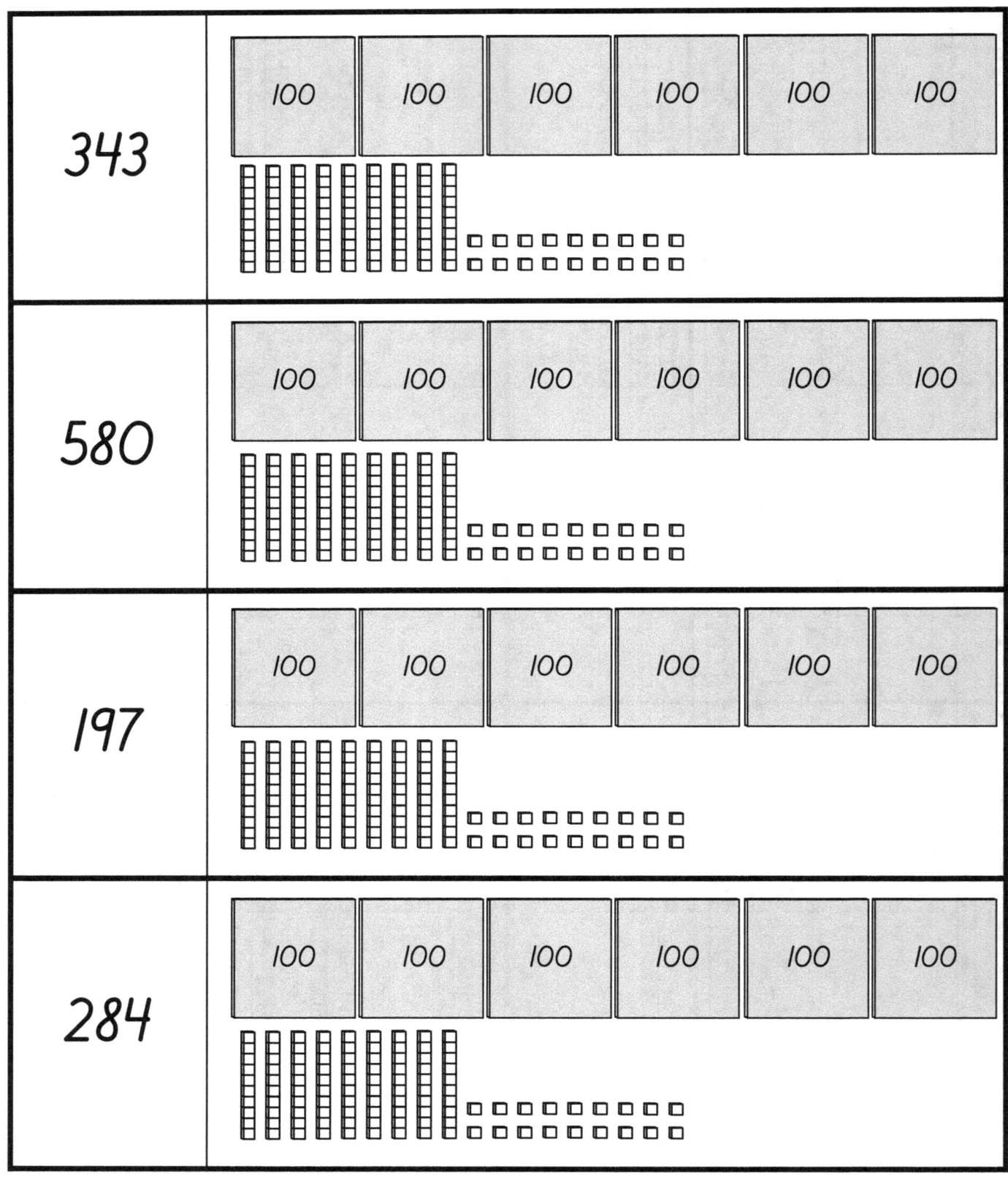

DRAW THE NUMBER

Draw boxes, sticks, and dots to represent the number shown.

248			754		
Hundreds	Tens	Ones	Hundreds	Tens	Ones

307			853		
Hundreds	Tens	Ones	Hundreds	Tens	Ones

652			341		
Hundreds	Tens	Ones	Hundreds	Tens	Ones

ADDITION

YUMMY ADDITION

Help the bakers find their cakes. Add the numbers to find the sum. Color the cake with the correct answer.

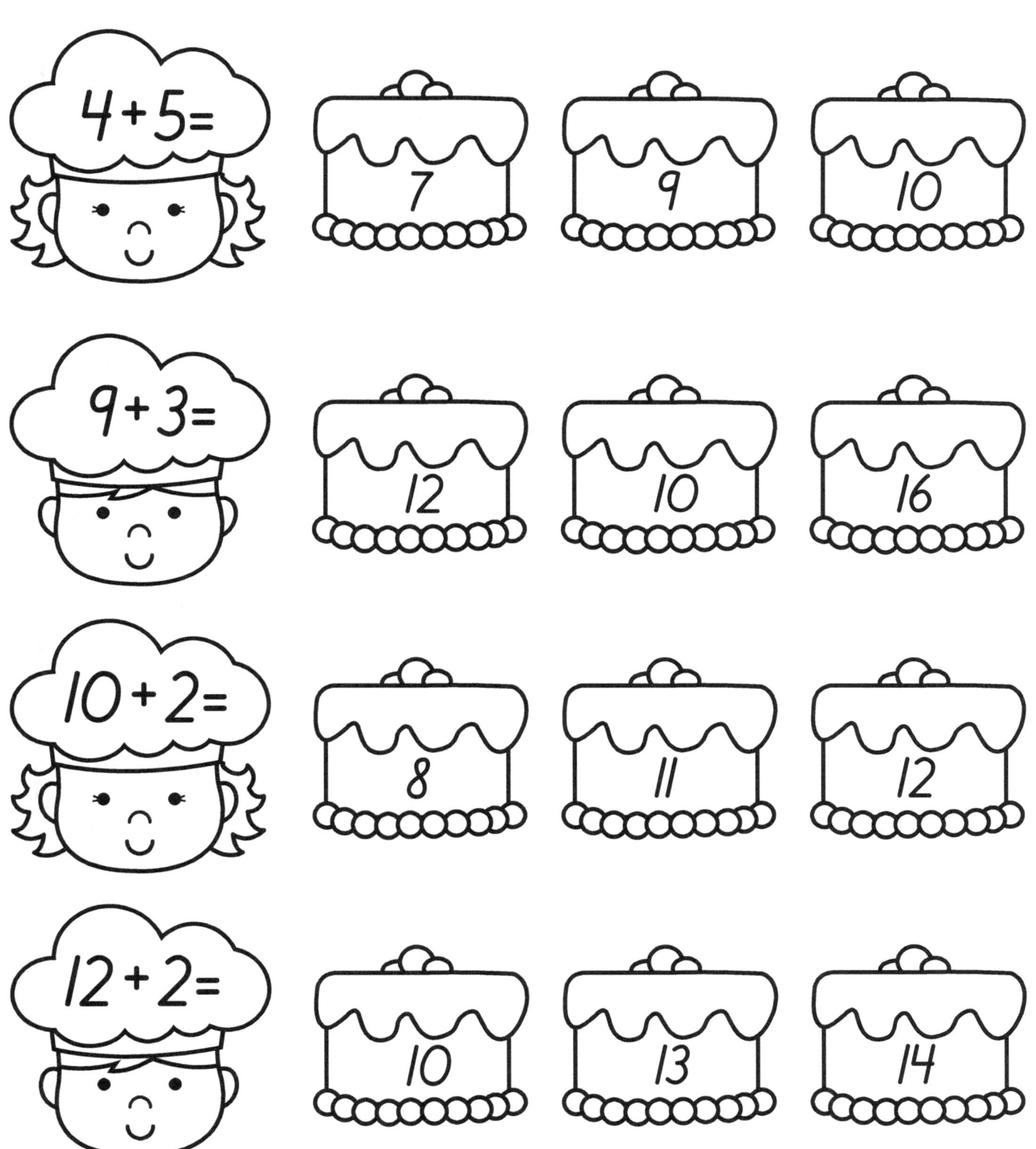

ADDITION MAZE

Make your way from start to "You Win" by answering the problem in the box and following the path with the correct answer. You may follow the path in any direction.

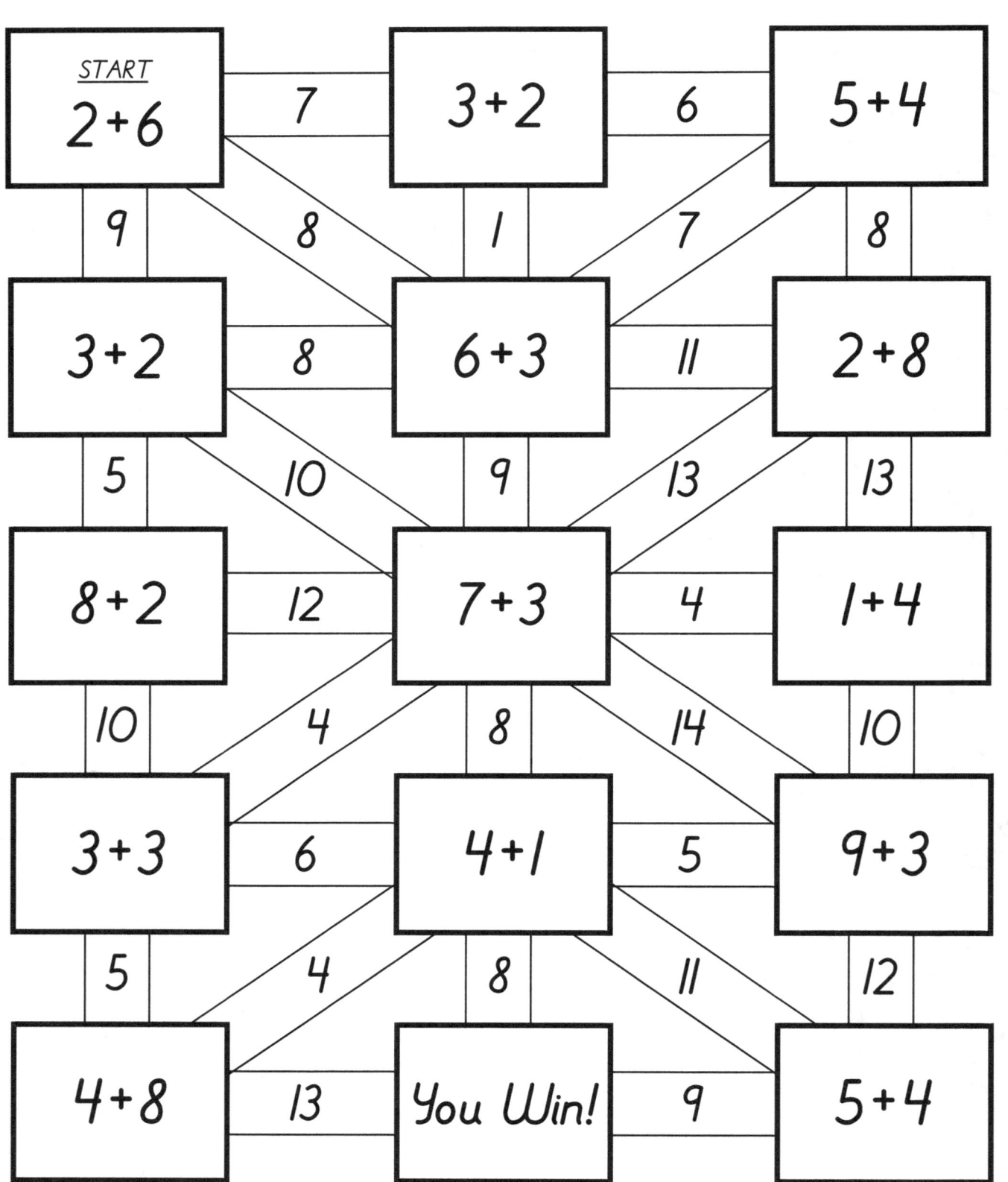

NUMBER PYRAMID

Look at the two numbers next to each other. Add the numbers together and write the answer in the box above them. Continue until you reach the top of the pyramid.

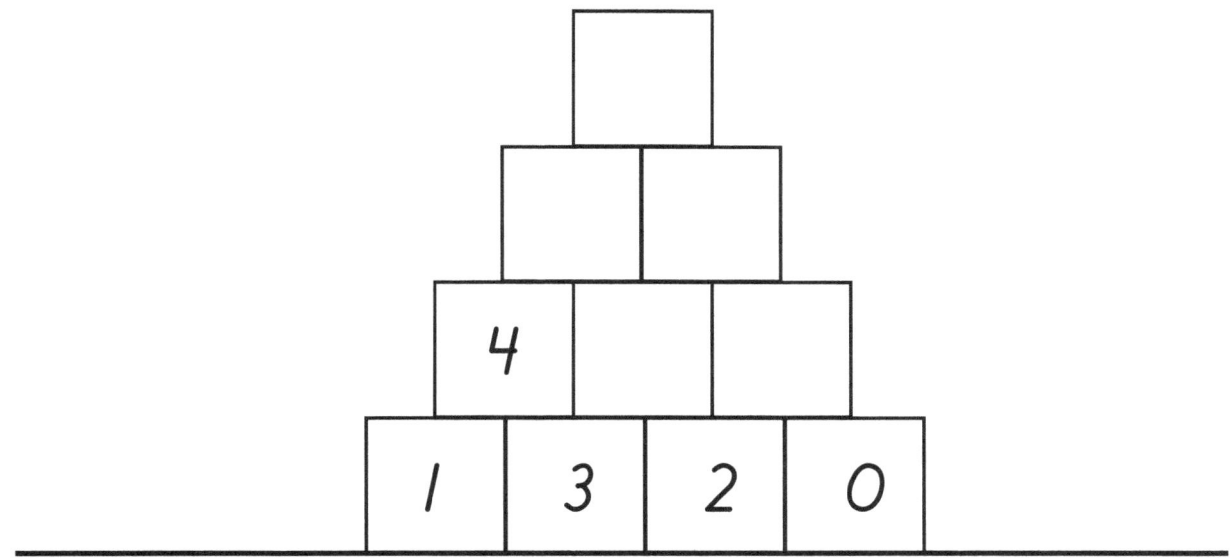

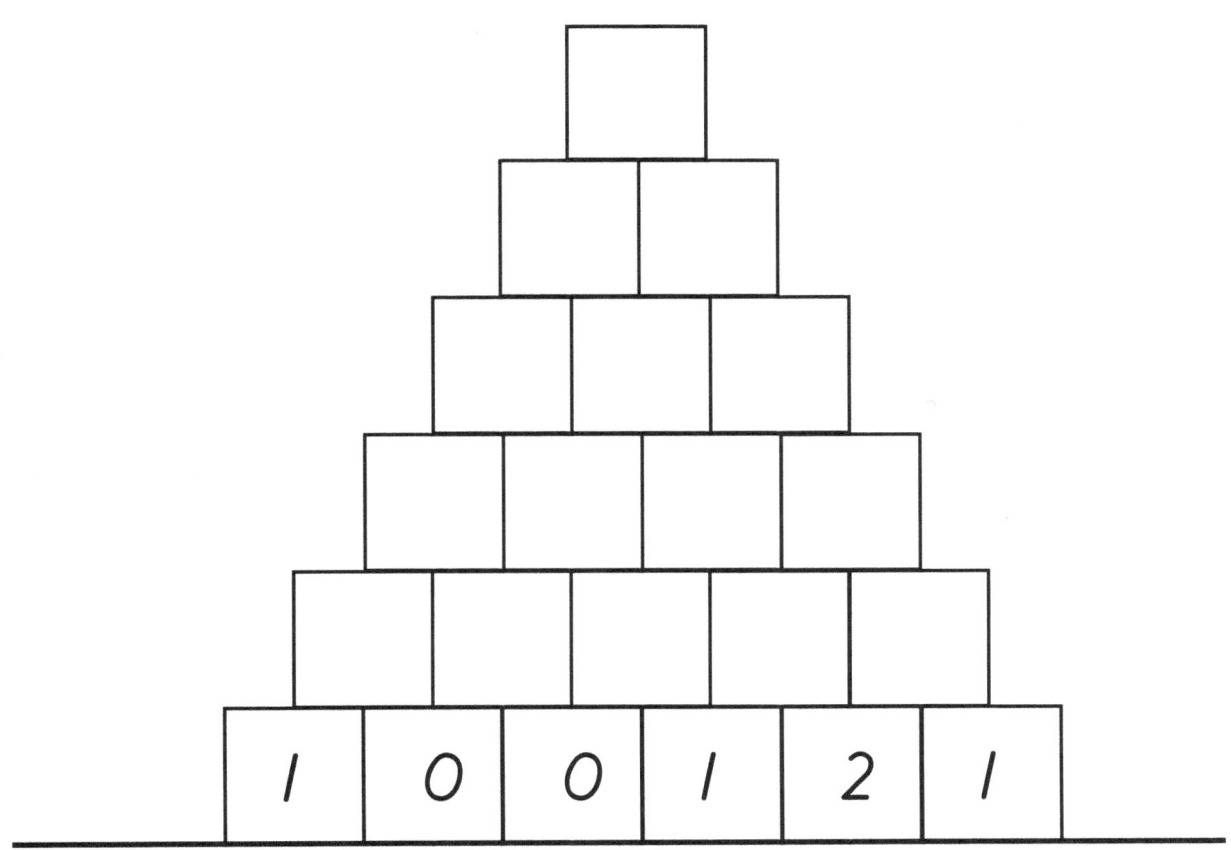

FACT FAMILIES

Use your french fries to write the fact family in the boxes for the below numbers.

1 2 3

1 + 2	=	3
2 + 1	=	3
3 − 2	=	1
3 − 1	=	2

2 3 5

+	=	
+	=	
−	=	
−	=	

3 4 7

+	=	
+	=	
−	=	
−	=	

4 2 6

+	=	
+	=	
−	=	
−	=	

5 3 8

+	=	
+	=	
−	=	
−	=	

5 4 9

+	=	
+	=	
−	=	
−	=	

ADDITION PUZZLE

Fill in the missing blanks.

[Addition crossword puzzle with the following equations to fill in:]

- 3 + 2 = ___
- ___ + 4 = 8
- ___ + 1 = ___
- ___ + 5 = ___
- 3 + 2 = ___ (vertical)
- ___ + ___ = ___
- 6 + ___ = ___ (vertical, with 2 below)
- ___ + ___ = 7
- ___ + ___ = 7
- 6 + ___ = 9
- 4 + ___ = 8
- ___ + 3 = ___
- ___ + 2 = ___ (vertical)
- ___ + 5 = ___ (vertical)
- ___ + ___ = ___

COLOR BY ADDITION

Solve each problem. Color by code.

10 = blue	6 = green	8 = brown
17 = orange	11 = purple	20 = red
12 = yellow	4 = pink	5 = light blue

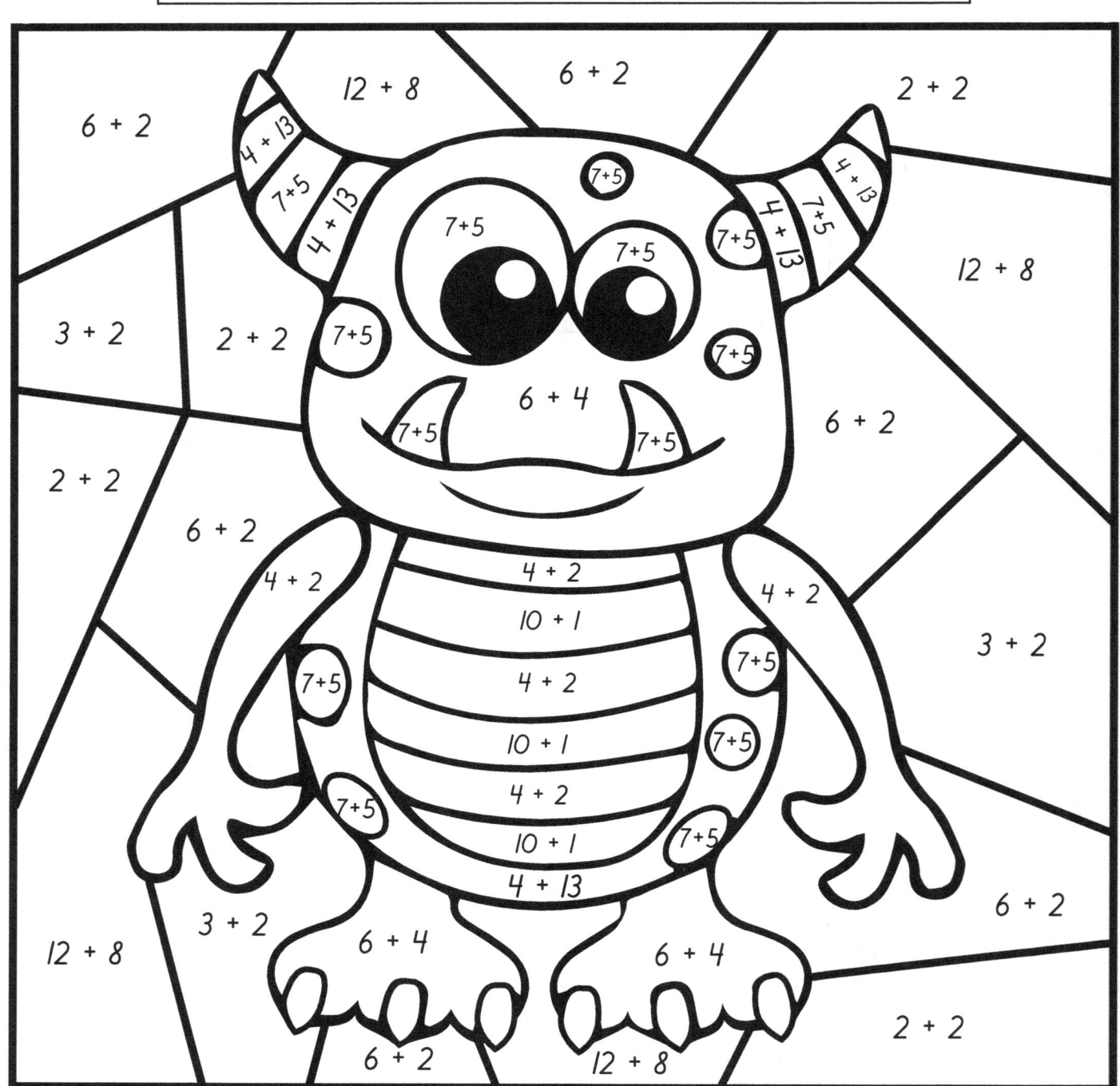

ADDITION PYRAMIDS 2

Look at the two numbers next to each other. Add the numbers together and write the answer in the box above them. Continue until you reach the top of the pyramid.

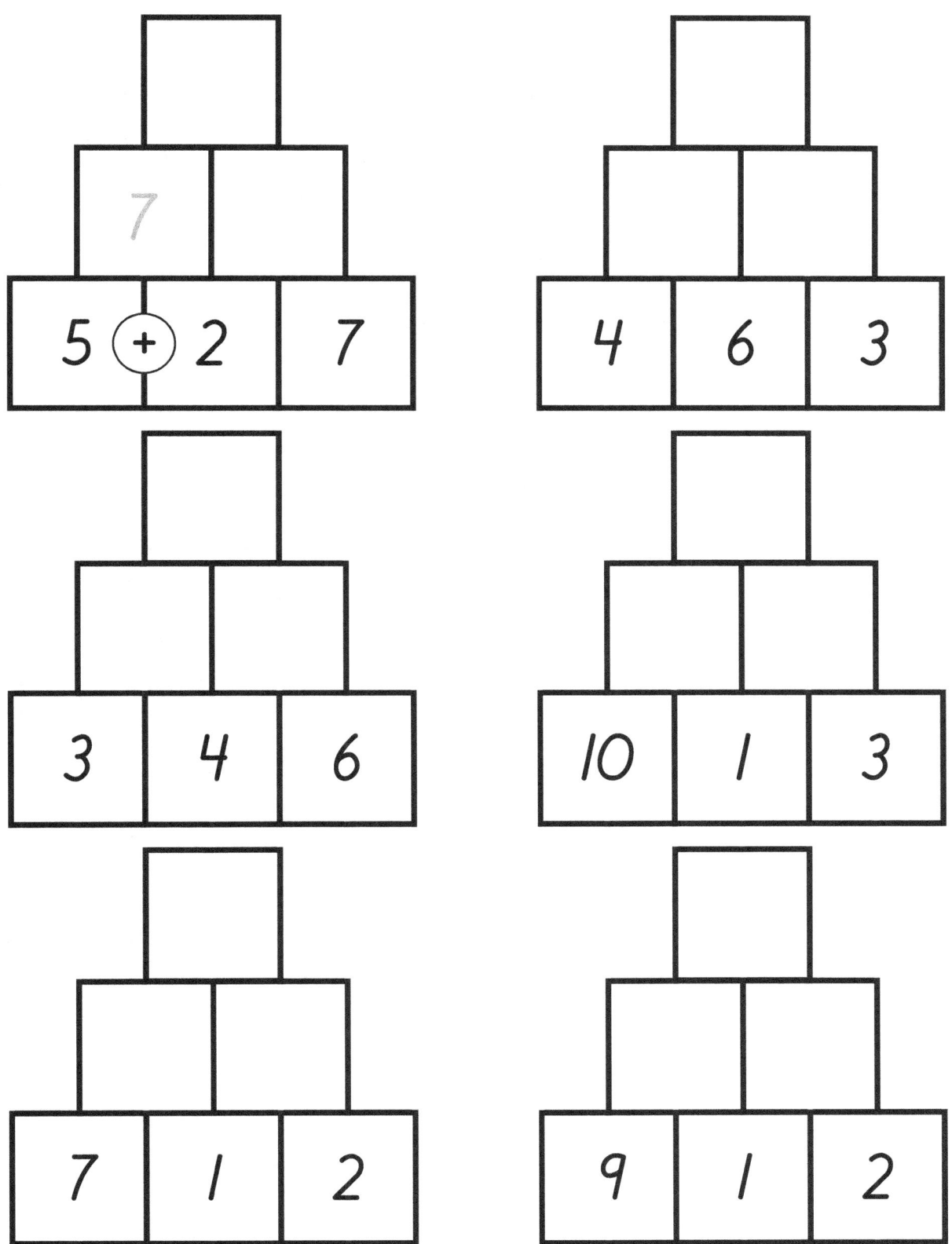

ADDITION RIDDLE

Solve each addition problem. Use the letters to answer the riddle at the bottom of the page.

What are pirates afraid of?

a: 14 + 2 = 16	e: 7 + 6 = 13	i: 8 + 5 = 13	o: 4 + 3 = 7	u: 8 + 6 = 14	y: 12 + 8 = 20
b: 2 + 9 = 11	c: 5 + 3 = 8	d: 4 + 5 = 9	f: 7 + 8 = 15	g: 3 + 9 = 12	h: 2 + 3 = 5
j: 6 + 7 = 13	k: 9 + 8 = 17	l: 9 + 7 = 16	m: 9 + 4 = 13	n: 1 + 2 = 3	q: 9 + 9 = 18
r: 6 + 6 = 12	s: 11 + 4 = 15	t: 6 + 4 = 10	v: 5 + 2 = 7	w: 5 + 6 = 11	x: 9 + 5 = 14

T H E   D A R R R K !
10 5 13   9 16 12 12 12 17

NUMBER LINE ADDITION

Use the number line to help you solve the addition sentence.

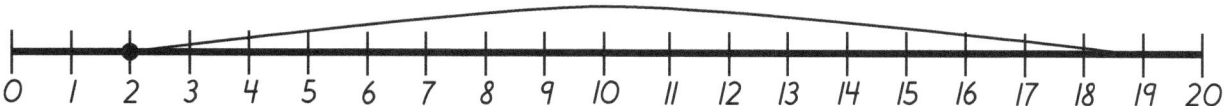

2 + 17 = 19

4 + 16 =

12 + 5 =

19 + 1 =

9 + 8 =

6 + 9 =

7 + 7 =

17 + 1 =

3 + 13 =

5 + 7 =

15 + 2 =

8 + 3 =

10 + 4 =

16 + 3 =

2-DIGIT ADDITION

Add using the blocks. Add the one blocks first and then the ten blocks.

Tens	Ones
2	4
+	3

Tens	Ones
3	5
+	4

Tens	Ones
5	3
+	2

Tens	Ones
4	1
+	5

Tens	Ones
3	4
+	4

Tens	Ones
2	5
+	3

Tens	Ones
6	3
+	1

Tens	Ones
5	2
+	6

ADDITION TIC-TAC-TOE

Play just like tic-tac-toe, but you must solve the problem before you can place an X or O.

$\begin{array}{r} 34 \\ +22 \\ \hline \end{array}$	$\begin{array}{r} 90 \\ +9 \\ \hline \end{array}$	$\begin{array}{r} 71 \\ +25 \\ \hline \end{array}$
$\begin{array}{r} 25 \\ +63 \\ \hline \end{array}$	$\begin{array}{r} 23 \\ +44 \\ \hline \end{array}$	$\begin{array}{r} 16 \\ +51 \\ \hline \end{array}$
$\begin{array}{r} 48 \\ +21 \\ \hline \end{array}$	$\begin{array}{r} 65 \\ +33 \\ \hline \end{array}$	$\begin{array}{r} 18 \\ +30 \\ \hline \end{array}$

MYSTERY NUMBER

Solve each addition problem. Read the clues at the bottom and cross out the wrong answers. Color the mystery number green.

16 +22	53 +33	10 +19	24 +71	52 +42
25 +31	20 +46	11 +8	16 +13	36 +31
84 +13	11 +11	43 +34	15 +10	66 +31
21 +16	36 +21	13 +13	31 +51	42 +26

Clue #1 - The mystery number does not have a 7 in the ones place.

Clue #2 - The mystery number has a 6 in it.

Clue #3 - The mystery number is greater than 30.

Clue #4 - The mystery number does not have an 8 in the tens place.

Clue #5 - When you add the two numbers in the mystery number together it equals 14.

DOUBLE DIGIT ADDITION

Solve each addition problem.

18 +31	42 +13	48 +11	16 +22
61 +62	22 +16	10 +71	53 +45
41 +34	21 +44	84 +15	61 +33
21 +44	41 +53	24 +53	GREAT!

SUBTRACTION

SUPER SUBTRACTION

Fill in the missing numbers to solve the problems.

$8 - \boxed{} = 6$ | $7 - \boxed{} = 3$

$\boxed{} - 3 = 2$ | $\boxed{} - 5 = 4$

$5 - \boxed{} = 1$ | $2 - \boxed{} = 0$

$\boxed{} - 2 = 7$ | $\boxed{} - 3 = 6$

$4 - \boxed{} = 3$ | $8 - \boxed{} = 4$

$\boxed{} - 6 = 2$ | $\boxed{} - 1 = 7$

$9 - \boxed{} = 5$ | $6 - \boxed{} = 4$

TRUE OR FALSE

Look at the equation. Is it correct? Circle if it is true or false.

8-7=6 True　　　False	7-5=2 True　　　False
9-4=5 True　　　False	6-5=1 True　　　False
10-3=7 True　　　False	5-2=1 True　　　False
7-6=3 True　　　False	10-6=4 True　　　False
10-5=4 True　　　False	8-8=0 True　　　False

NUMBER LINE SUBTRACTION

Use the number line to help you solve the subtraction sentence.

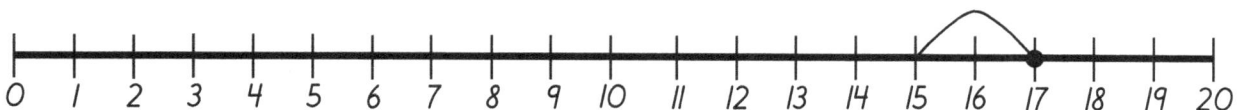

17 - 2 = 15   20 - 15 =

12 - 6 =   19 - 8 =

18 - 4 =   11 - 5 =

13 - 3 =   16 - 1 =

19 - 10 =   13 - 8 =

14 - 5 =   18 - 9 =

17 + 12 =   20 - 13 =

COLOR BY SUBTRACTION

Solve each problem. Color by code.

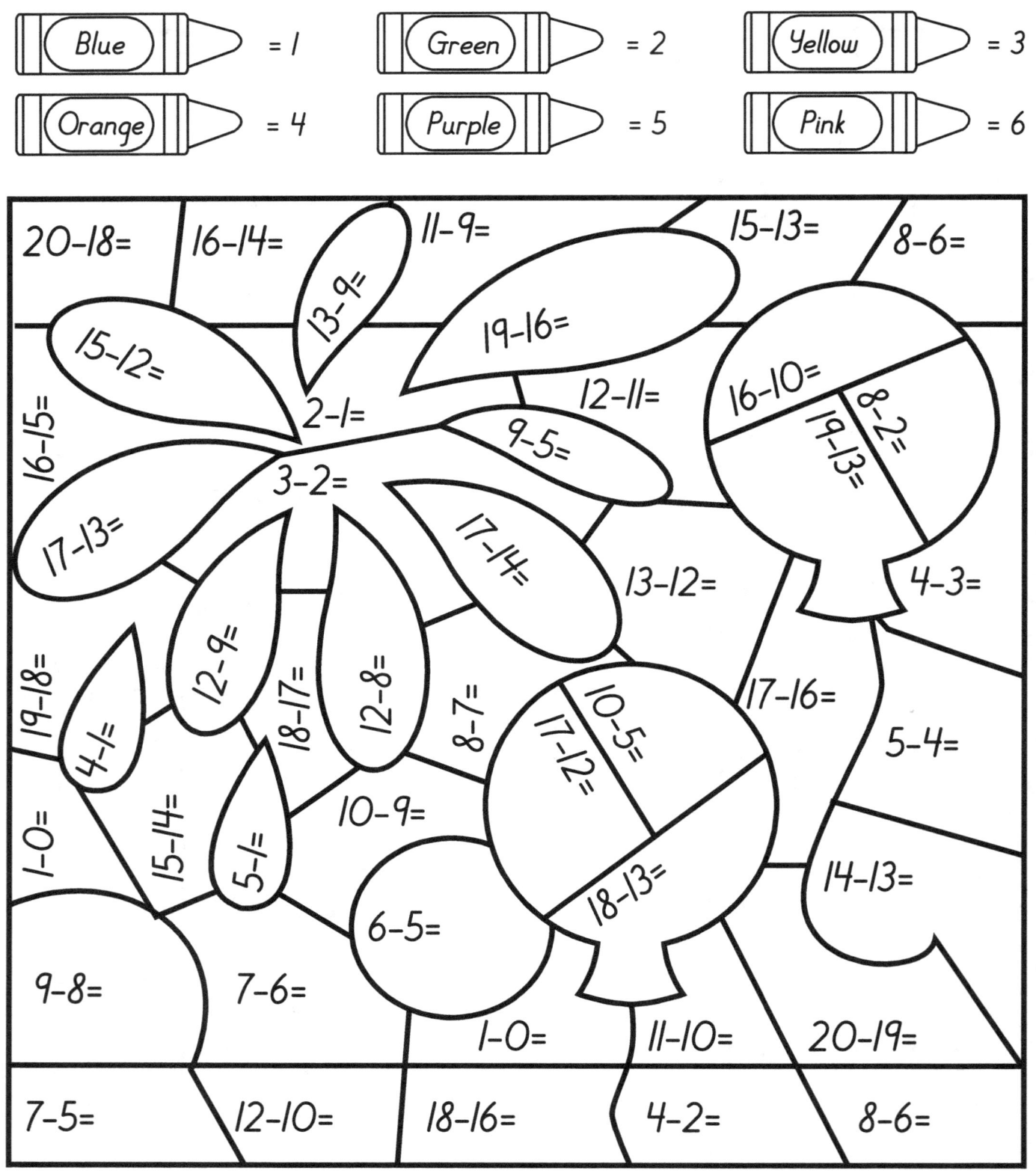

BLOCK SUBTRACTION

Cross out the blocks to solve the problem. Write your answer.

19 −3 = 16	16 −2 =
18 −6 =	11 −1 =
13 −2 =	17 −2 =
15 −4 =	19 −6 =
18 −3 =	14 −1 =

Learning 1st Grade Math Workbook | Autumn McKay

SUBTRACTION MAZE

Make your way from start to "You Win" by answering the problem in the box and following the path with the correct answer. You may follow the path in any direction.

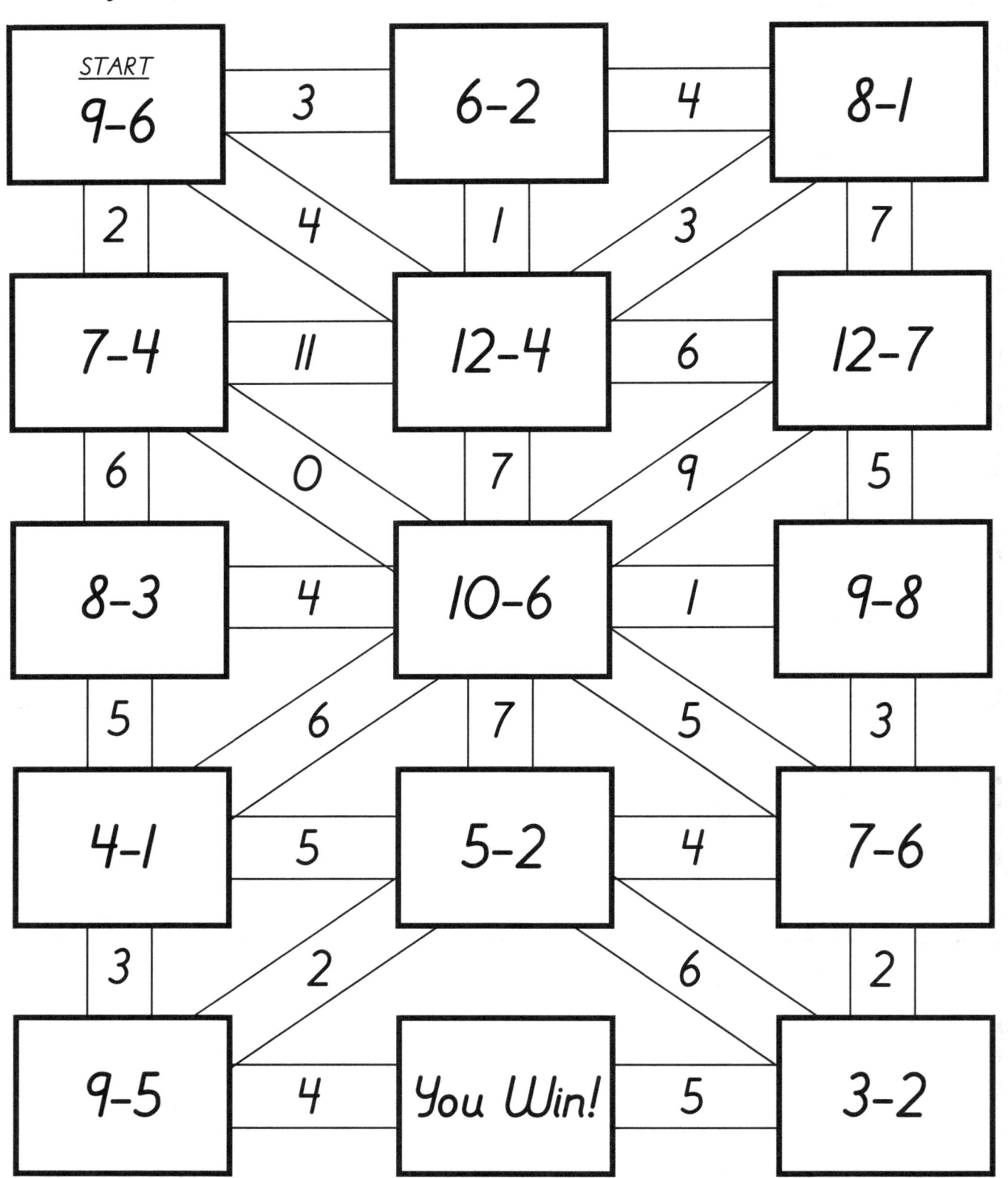

SUBTRACTION RIDDLE

Solve each subtraction problem. Use the letters to answer the riddle at the bottom of the page.

What kind of meals do math teachers eat?

a: 12 − 8	e: 6 − 4	i: 11 − 5	o: 12 − 9	u: 2 − 1	y: 14 − 5
b: 7 − 4	c: 11 − 8	d: 6 − 3	f: 11 − 0	g: 13 − 7	h: 10 − 4
j: 9 − 3	k: 17 − 5	l: 10 − 0	m: 16 − 2	n: 8 − 5	q: 20 − 5
r: 14 − 9	s: 15 − 8	t: 3 − 3	v: 8 − 0	w: 18 − 10	x: 19 − 7

__ __ __ __ __ __   __ __ __ __ __ !
7 15 1 4 5 2   14 2 4 10 7

SUBTRACTION AND ADDITION PUZZLE

Fill in the missing blanks.

SUBTRACTING TENS

Cross out the tens to solve the equation. Write the answer.

20-10=	60-30=	50-30=	90-40=
40-20=	70-30=	30-10=	80-70=
60-10=	50-10=	60-40=	50-40=

Learning 1st Grade Math Workbook | Autumn McKay

SUBTRACTING TENS 2

Cross out the tens to solve the equation. Write the answer.

64 - 30 =	71 - 20 =
55 - 10 =	44 - 40 =
96 - 10 =	28 - 10 =
67 - 50 =	34 - 20 =

BLOCK SUBTRACTION 2

Cross out the tens and ones to solve the equation. Cross out the one blocks first and then the ten blocks.

Tens	Ones
4	5
-2	3
2	2

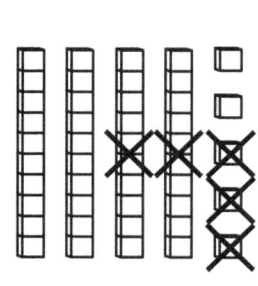

Tens	Ones
2	6
-1	1

Tens	Ones
5	4
-4	2

Tens	Ones
4	5
-1	3

Tens	Ones
7	5
-3	0

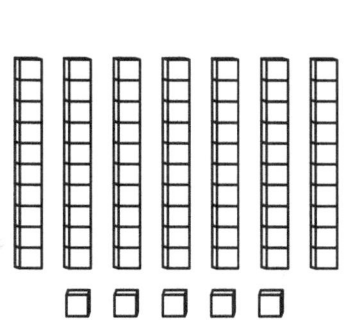

Tens	Ones
6	5
-3	1

Tens	Ones
2	8
-1	3

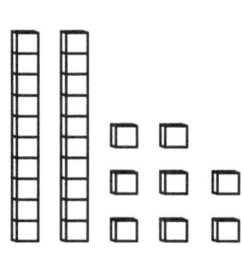

Tens	Ones
6	6
-1	4

SUBTRACTION PRACTICE

Solve the subtraction problems.

89 -42	66 -35	78 -25	56 -24	65 -31
93 -52	88 -65	38 -13	45 -34	91 -20
83 -42	77 -14	76 -34	49 -22	38 -21
85 -24	56 -31	88 -14		

SUBTRACTION PRACTICE 2

Solve the subtraction problems.

989 -654	776 -543	665 -432	654 -321
543 -210	963 -852	852 -651	759 -426
846 -324	977 -354	459 -324	786 -462
684 -241	954 -324	684 -242	862 -221
	974 -653	866 -254	

MONEY

PENNY

The penny is copper. It is worth 1 cent. Abraham Lincoln was the 16th President of the United States of America. He is on the penny.

Trace the word below.

penny   penny   penny

Color the penny.

front

back

Count and add up all of the coins.

🪙 = _____ ¢

🪙🪙🪙 = _____ ¢

🪙🪙 = _____ ¢

NICKEL

The nickel is silver. It is worth 5 cents. Thomas Jefferson was the 3rd President of the United States of America. He is on the front of the nickel.

Trace the word below.

nickel   nickel   nickel

Color the nickel.

 front

 back

Count and add up all of the coins.

= _____ ¢

= _____ ¢

= _____ ¢

DIME

The dime is silver. It is worth 10 cents. It is our smallest coin. Franklin Roosevelt was the 32nd President of the United States of America. He is on the front of the dime.

Trace the word below.

dime   dime   dime

Color the dime.

front

back

Count and add up all of the coins.

= ____ ¢

= ____ ¢

= ____ ¢

Learning 1st Grade Math Workbook | Autumn McKay

QUARTER

The quarter is silver. It is worth 25 cents. George Washington was the 1st President of the United States of America. He is on front of the quarter.

Trace the word below.

quarter   quarter

Color the quarter.

 front

 back

Count and add up all of the coins.

= _____ ¢

= _____ ¢

= _____ ¢

DOLLAR

The dollar is green. It is worth $1, 4 quarters, 10 dimes, 20 nickels or 100 pennies. George Washington is on the front of the dollar just like the quarter.

Trace the word below.

dollar   dollar   dollar

Color the dollar.

 front

 back

Count and add up all of the dollars.

= _____ $

= _____ $

= _____ $

Learning 1st Grade Math Workbook | Autumn McKay

COLOR BY COIN

Use the code to color the coins.

Penny — red
Nickel — blue
Dime — green
Quarter — purple

MONEY MATCH

Draw a line to match the coins to the correct total.

1.    A. 36 ¢

2.    B. 27 ¢

3.    C. 31 ¢

4.    D. 35 ¢

5.    E. 45 ¢

6.    F. 30 ¢

7.    G. 20 ¢

8.    H. 16 ¢

9.    I. 12 ¢

10.    J. 7 ¢

COUNTING COINS

Write the amount of money inside each piggy bank.

 1 ¢ 5 ¢ 10 ¢ 25 ¢

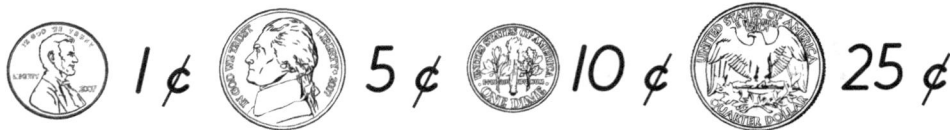

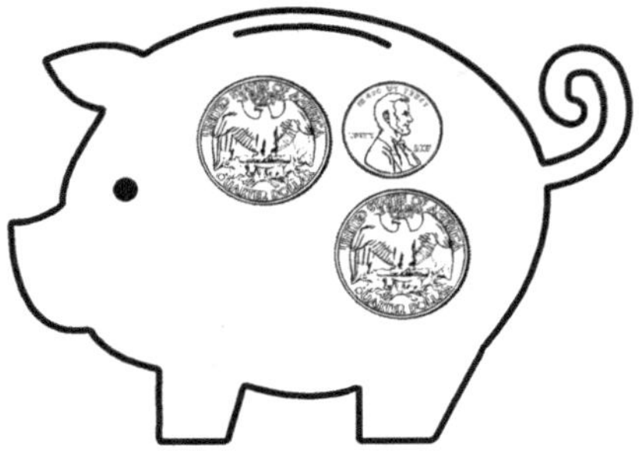

How much? 51 ¢

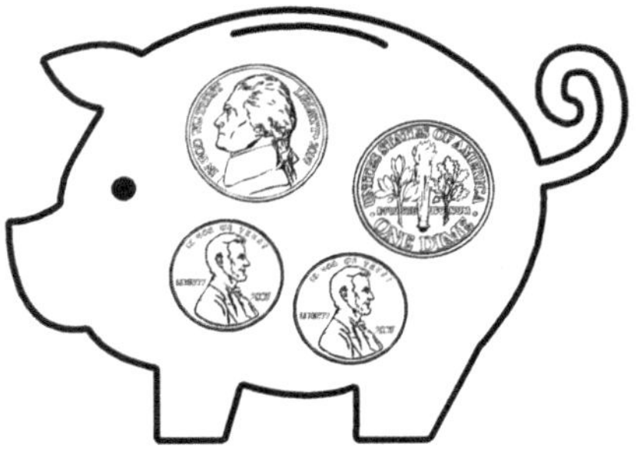

How much? ____________

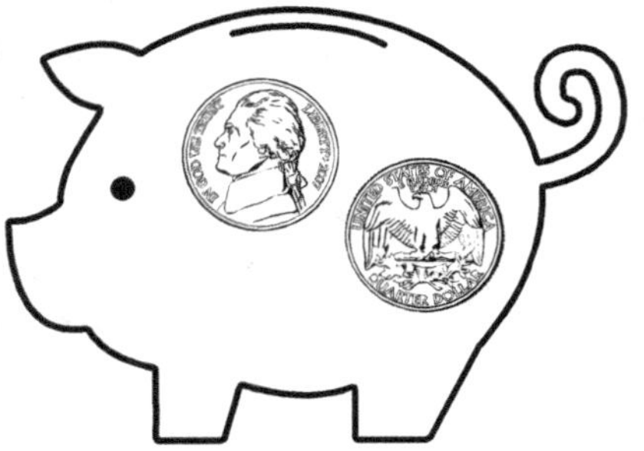

How much? ____________

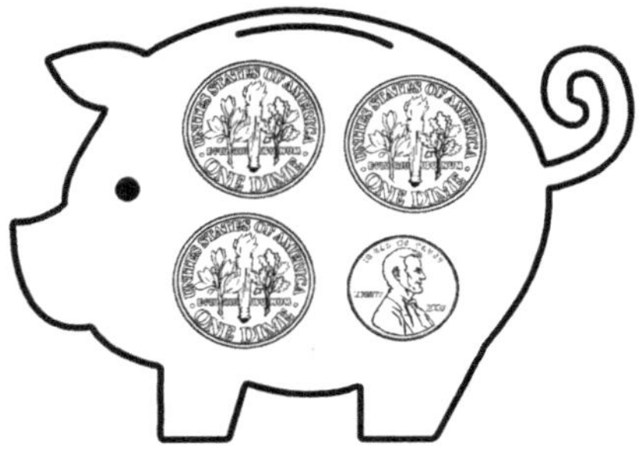

How much? ____________

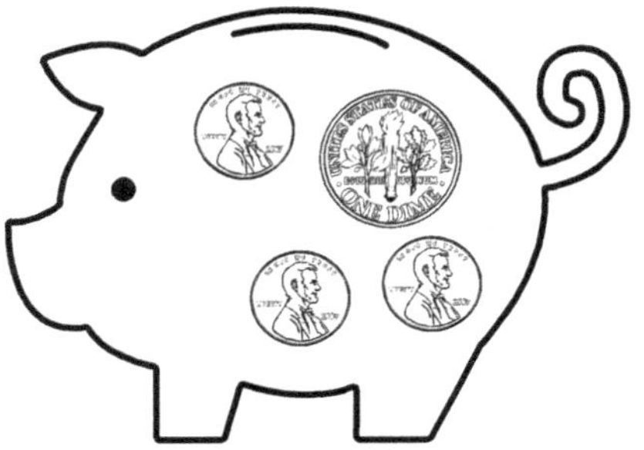

How much? ____________

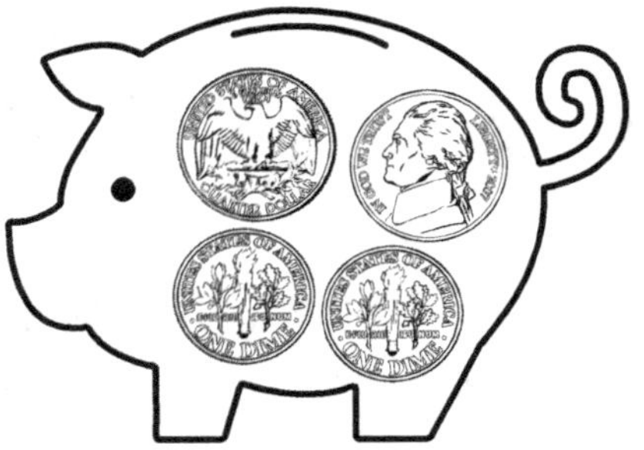

How much? ____________

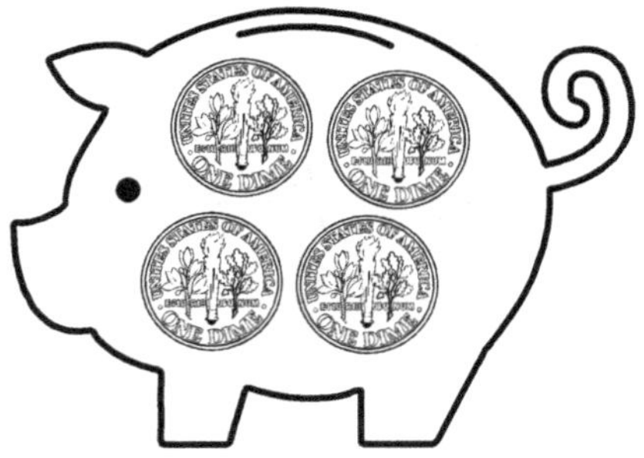

How much? ____________

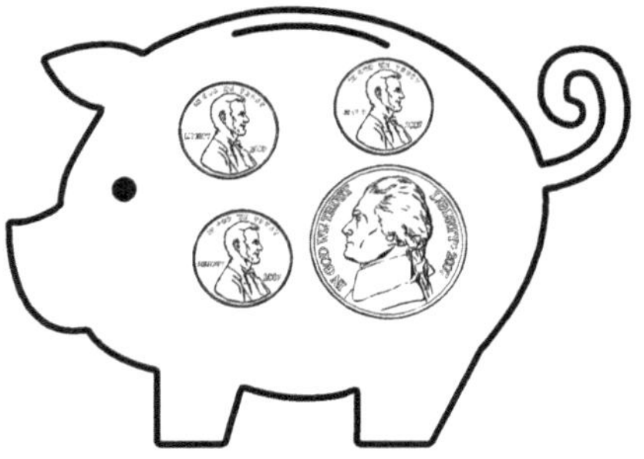

How much? ____________

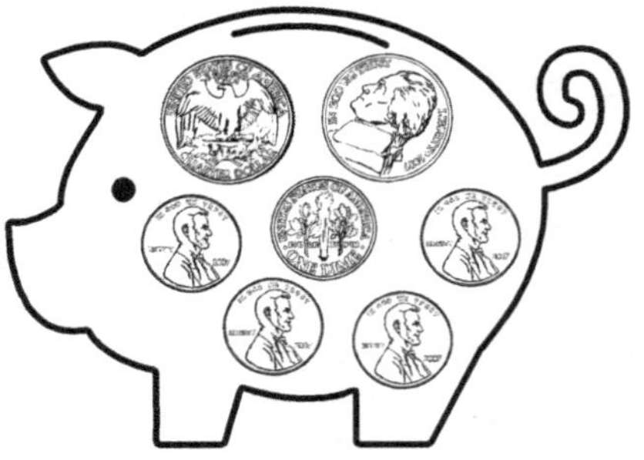

How much? ____________

WHICH ONE CAN YOU BUY?

Color the fruit you can buy based on the coins you have.

Coins	Fruit Choices
4 dimes, 2 nickels, 1 penny	watermelon 41¢ / bananas 51¢
3 dimes, 3 nickels, 2 pennies	lemon 62¢ / pear 47¢
5 dimes, 2 pennies	cherries 72¢ / lemon 52¢
5 dimes, 3 nickels, 3 pennies	grapes 68¢ / plum 83¢
3 dimes, 3 nickels, 3 pennies	raspberry 58¢ / orange 83¢

MAKE IT MATCH

Color the coins to equal the number shown on the left.

56 ¢	quarter quarter quarter dime dime nickel nickel penny penny
70 ¢	quarter quarter quarter dime dime nickel nickel penny penny
47 ¢	quarter quarter quarter dime dime nickel nickel penny penny
66 ¢	quarter quarter quarter dime dime nickel nickel penny penny
82 ¢	quarter quarter quarter dime dime nickel nickel penny penny
51 ¢	quarter quarter quarter dime dime nickel nickel penny penny
67 ¢	quarter quarter quarter dime dime nickel nickel penny penny
46 ¢	quarter quarter quarter dime dime nickel nickel penny penny

WHO HAS MORE?

Count the money next to each child. Write the amount in the box. Color the child with the most money.

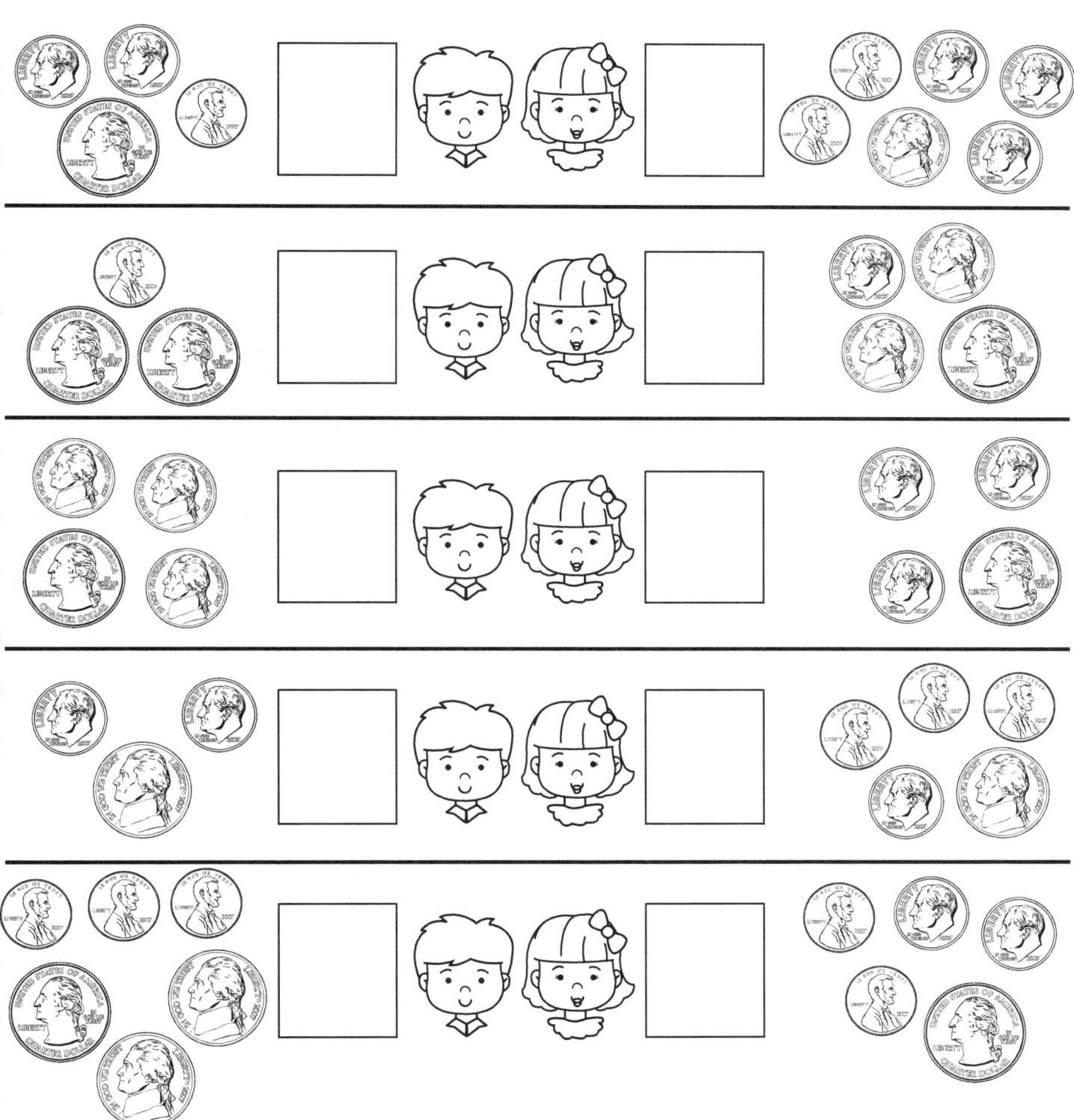

CAN YOU BUY IT?

Do you have enough money to buy each item? Draw a smiley face in the box if you do. Draw a frowny face in the box if you do not.

MONEY ADDITION

Add the money together, and write the amount.

TIME

MAKE A CLOCK

Cut and paste the minutes around the clock in the correct order. Paste the hour hand and minute hand in the center of the clock.

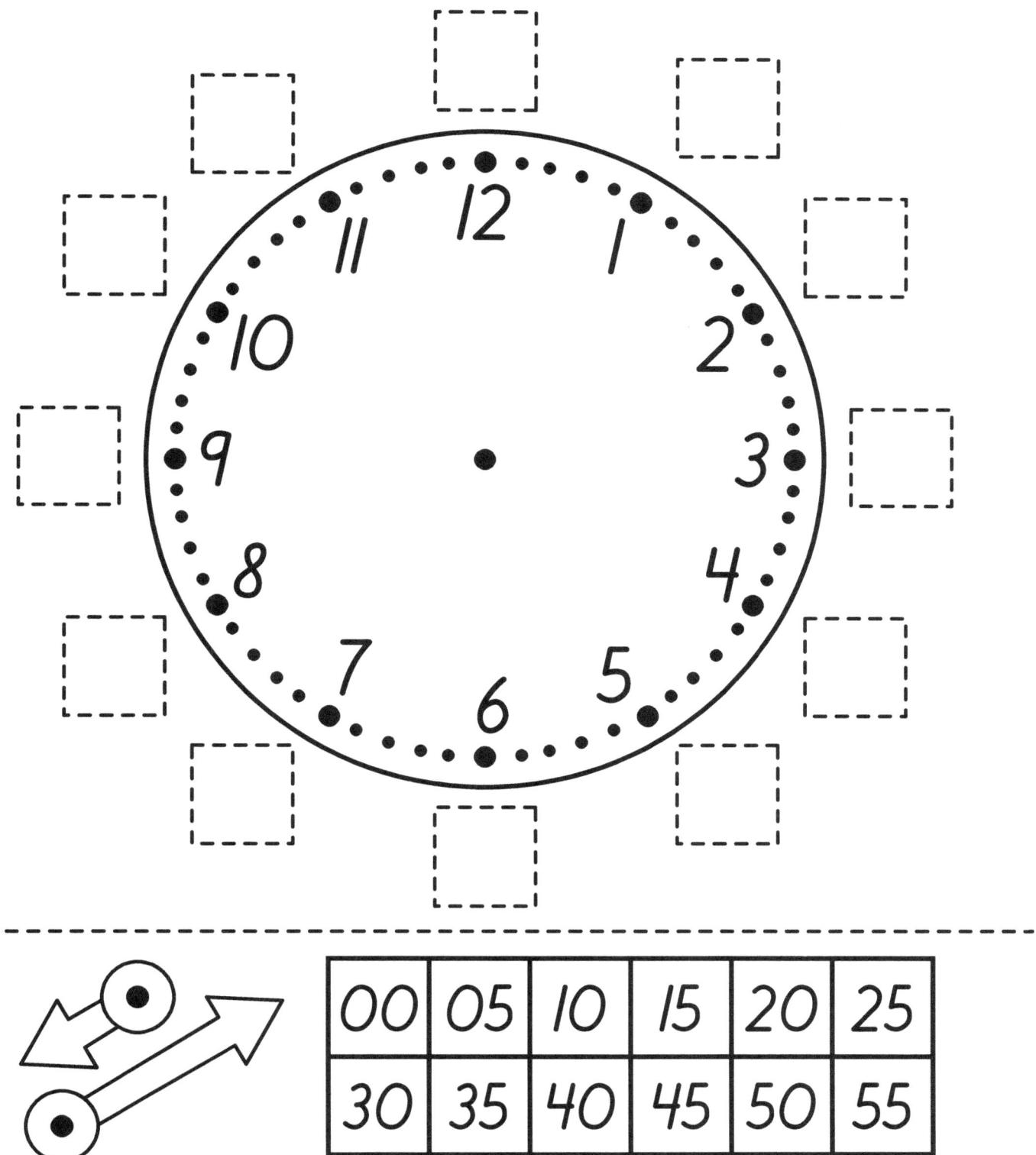

00	05	10	15	20	25
30	35	40	45	50	55

Learning 1st Grade Math Workbook | Autumn McKay

COLOR THE WATCH

Read the directions and color.

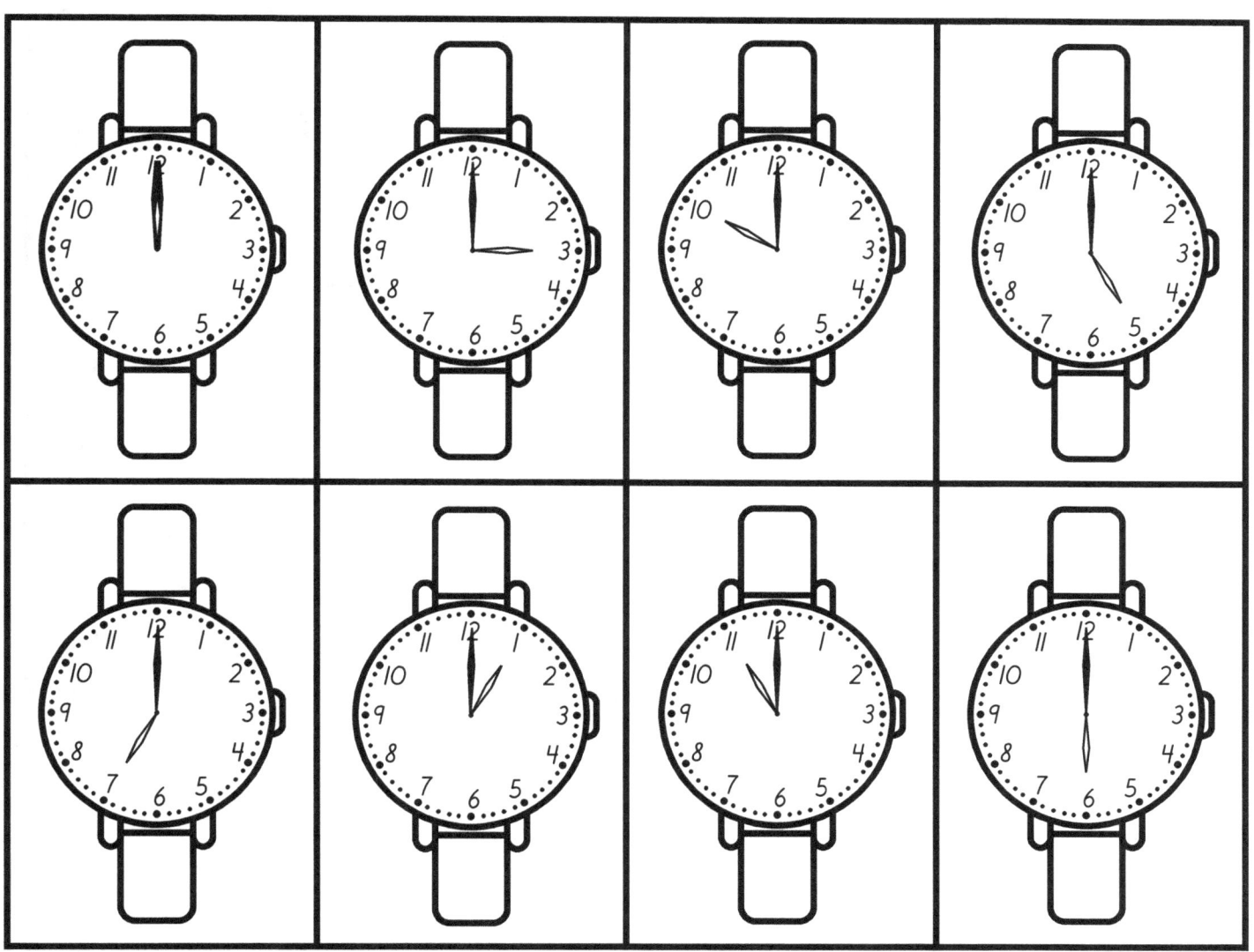

Color the watch that shows 12:00 red.
Color the watch that shows 5:00 green.
Color the watch that shows 6:00 yellow.
Color the watch that shows 3:00 purple.
Color the watch that shows 11:00 blue.
Color the watch that shows 7:00 orange.
Color the watch that shows 1:00 brown.
Color the watch that shows 10:00 pink..

SCHOOL TIME

Color the clock that shows the correct time for each activity.

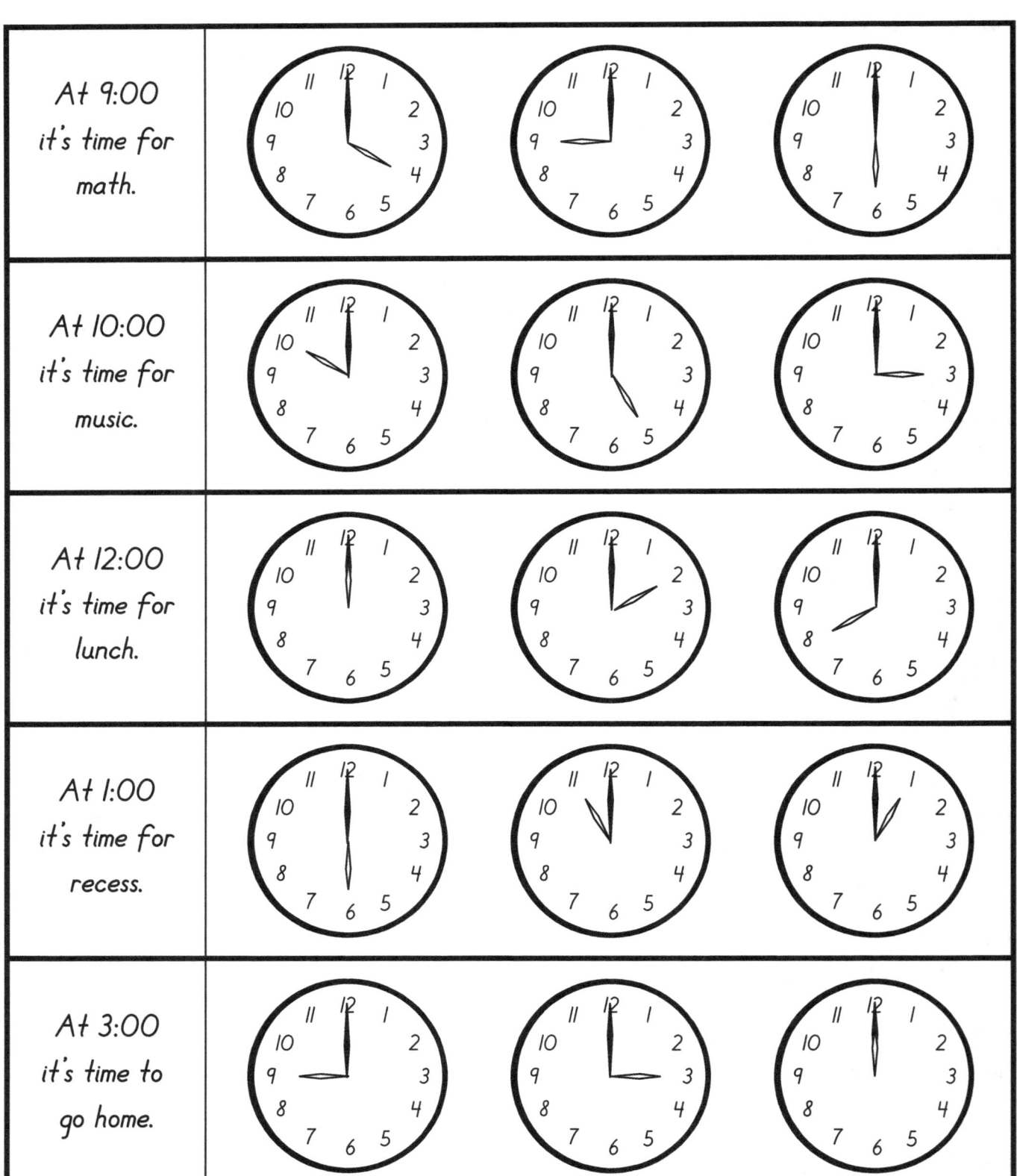

DRAW THE HANDS

Look at the digital times for each clock. Draw hands on the clock to show the correct time.

8:30	2:30	10:30	1:30
11:30	9:30	3:30	6:30
12:30	4:30	7:30	5:30

WRITE THE TIME

Write the time shown on each clock in the space provided.

2 : 30	11 : 00	12 : 30
7 : 30	9 : 30	10 : 30
12 : 00	6 : 30	4 : 30

TIME RIDDLE

Write the time for each clock. Use the letters to answer the riddle at the bottom of the page.

What time is it when you find an elephant in your car?

a	e	i	o	u	y
:	:	:	:	:	:
b	**c**	**d**	**f**	**g**	**h**
:	:	:	:	:	:
j	**k**	**l**	**m**	**n**	**p**
:	:	:	:	:	:
r	**s**	**t**	**v**	**w**	**x**
:	:	:	:	:	:

___ ___ ___ ___   ___ ___   ___ ___ ___
7:30 1:00 3:30 5:30 7:30 9:00 2:00 5:30 7:30

___   ___ ___ ___   ___ ___ ___ !
2:30 8:00 5:30 1:30 6:00 2:30 7:00

TELLING TIME

Draw the hour and minute hand on each clock to show the correct time.

Clock	Time	Clock	Time
	= 12:15		= 8:00
	= 8:30		= 6:30
	= 2:00		= 7:45
	= 3:45		= 7:00
	= 4:00		= 2:30
	= 1:15		= 9:45

MATCH THE TIME

View the time on the clocks. Draw a line from the digital time to the correct time on the clock.

7:15

2:30

11:45

9:00

1:15

5:30

12:45

4:00

6:15

10:30

3:45

8:00

Learning 1st Grade Math Workbook | Autumn McKay

ACTIVITY TIMES

Look at the picture and the clock. What time did the activity happen? Write the time.

WHAT TIME IS IT?

Write the time shown on the clock in the blank.

FRACTIONS

SILLY SHAPES

Color the shapes divided into equal parts purple. Color the shapes divided into unequal parts yellow.

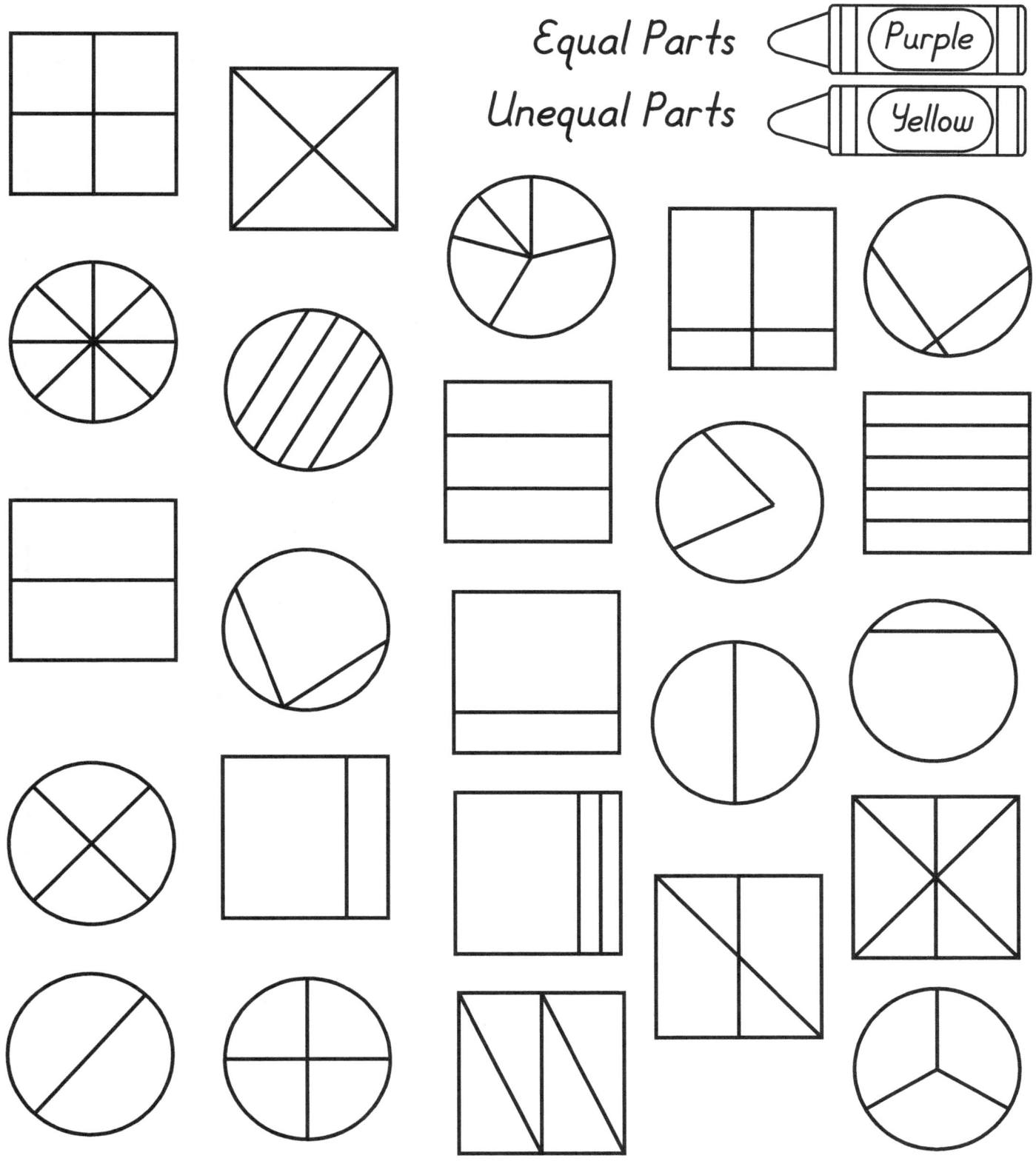

HALVES

Halves are the 2 equal parts of a whole.

Color the shapes that have been cut into half:

Cut these shapes into half:

Color one half of each shape:

FRACTIONS

Color the correct fraction of each shape.

Color $\frac{1}{2}$			
Color $\frac{1}{4}$			
Color $\frac{2}{3}$			
Color $\frac{2}{4}$			
Color $\frac{3}{4}$			

PIZZA FRACTIONS

Read the directions below to make the perfect pizza. Each piece of pizza gets only one type of topping.

Follow the steps below to make the perfect pizza.

1. Add sauce to the whole pizza.

2. Add pepperoni to 4/8 of the pizza.

3. Add mushrooms to 1/8 of the pizza.

4. Add ham to 2/8 of the pizza.

5. Add pineapple to 1/8 of the pizza.

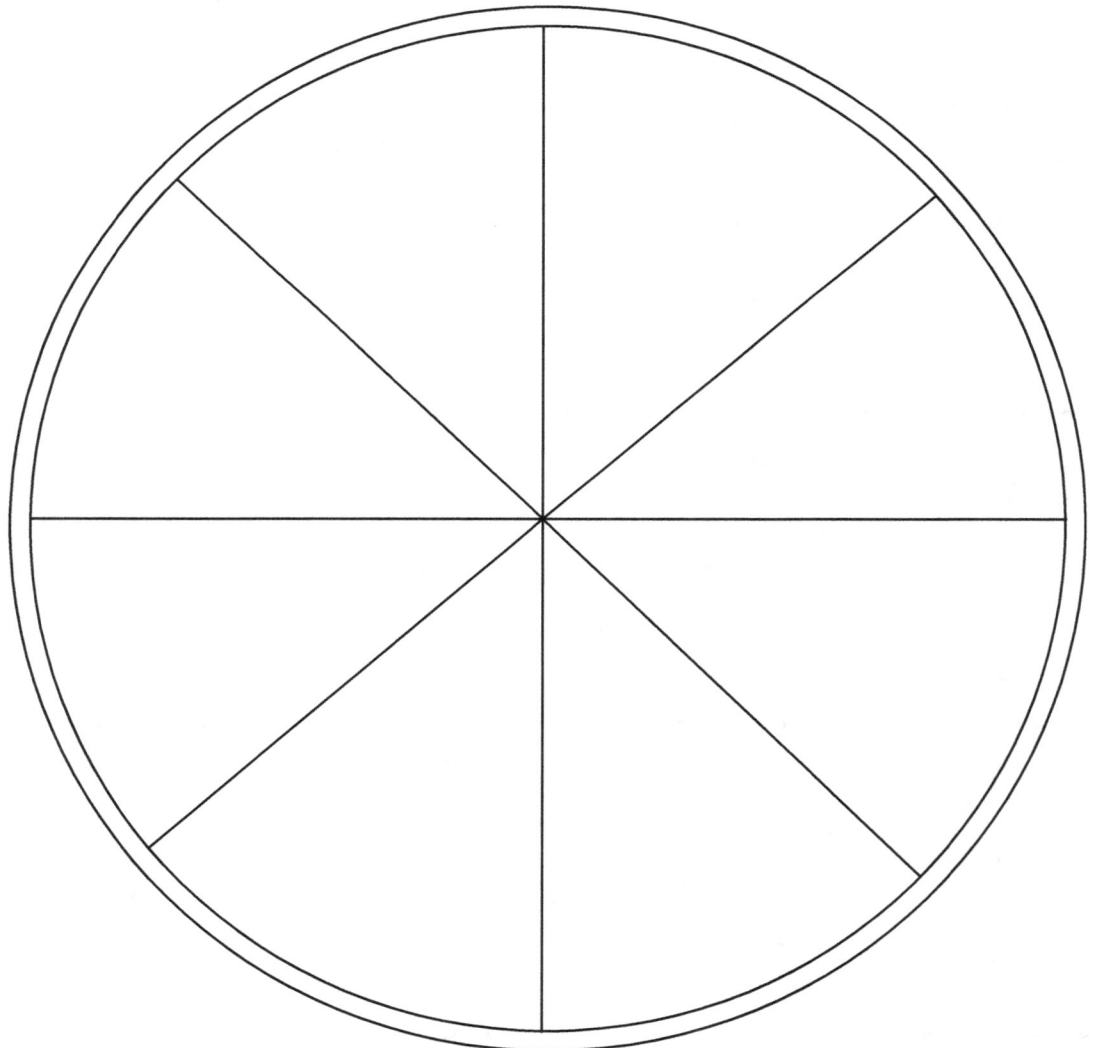

BUG FRACTIONS

Color in each bug with the fraction shown below.

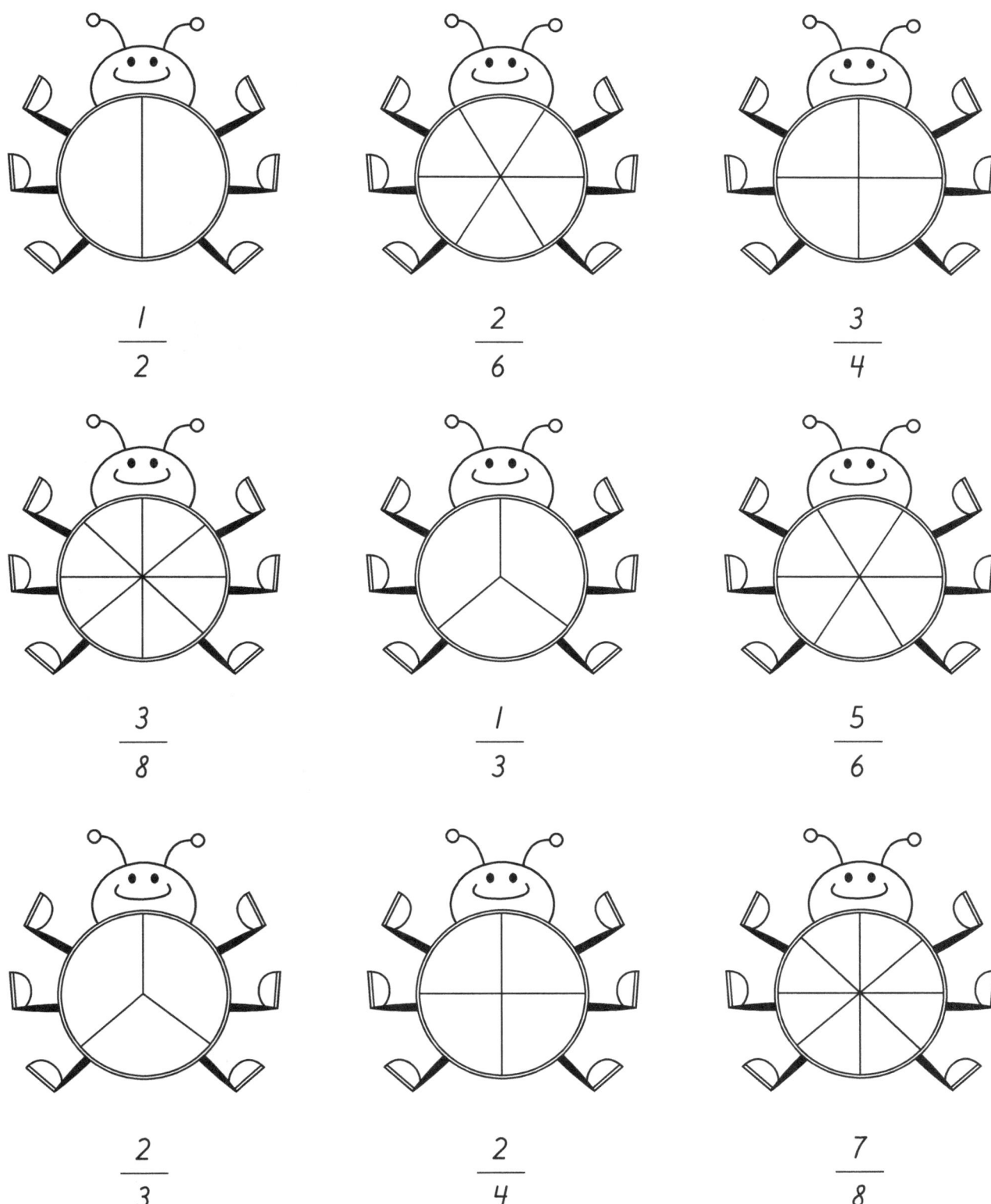

COLOR THE FRACTIONS

Color each circle with the fraction shown.

○	Color $\frac{1}{4}$	○	Color $\frac{2}{5}$
○	Color $\frac{1}{3}$	○	Color $\frac{1}{5}$
○	Color $\frac{2}{4}$	○	Color $\frac{3}{4}$
○	Color $\frac{2}{3}$	○	Color $\frac{4}{5}$
○	Color $\frac{3}{5}$	○	Color $\frac{1}{2}$

FRUIT FRACTIONS

Color the correct amount of fruit to represent the fraction shown.

Color $\frac{3}{4}$

Color $\frac{5}{6}$

Color $\frac{2}{5}$

Color $\frac{5}{7}$

Color $\frac{6}{8}$

Color $\frac{2}{3}$

Learning 1st Grade Math Workbook | Autumn McKay

MORE PIZZA FRACTIONS

Chef Tony needs to get 15 pizzas ready for a big party. Help him by adding the pepperoni pieces. The fraction shows how much of the pizza needs pepperoni pieces. Draw small, round red circles for the pepperoni. Chef Tony did the first pizza for you.

$\frac{1}{2}$	$\frac{3}{4}$	$\frac{2}{6}$
$\frac{1}{3}$	$\frac{6}{8}$	$\frac{2}{4}$
$\frac{5}{6}$	$\frac{2}{8}$	$\frac{4}{6}$
$\frac{3}{6}$	$\frac{3}{8}$	$\frac{1}{4}$
$\frac{2}{3}$	$\frac{1}{6}$	$\frac{7}{8}$

PICK THE RIGHT FRACTION

Look at the image on the left. The shaded part represents a fraction. Circle the correct fraction it represents.

⊕	$\frac{1}{2}$	$\frac{3}{6}$	(⃝$\frac{5}{6}$)	$\frac{1}{6}$	$\frac{5}{6}$
⊕	$\frac{1}{4}$	$\frac{3}{4}$	$\frac{1}{6}$	$\frac{1}{3}$	$\frac{1}{5}$
▦	$\frac{1}{2}$	$\frac{3}{8}$	$\frac{1}{6}$	$\frac{1}{7}$	$\frac{6}{8}$
⊠	$\frac{1}{3}$	$\frac{3}{6}$	$\frac{1}{2}$	$\frac{1}{5}$	$\frac{1}{4}$
⊕	$\frac{4}{6}$	$\frac{5}{6}$	$\frac{4}{5}$	$\frac{1}{6}$	$\frac{3}{5}$
◺	$\frac{1}{3}$	$\frac{1}{4}$	$\frac{1}{2}$	$\frac{1}{5}$	$\frac{2}{1}$
△	$\frac{1}{2}$	$\frac{3}{4}$	$\frac{5}{6}$	$\frac{1}{4}$	$\frac{4}{3}$
⊕	$\frac{1}{6}$	$\frac{2}{3}$	$\frac{3}{3}$	$\frac{1}{3}$	$\frac{2}{5}$
▤	$\frac{3}{5}$	$\frac{3}{4}$	$\frac{5}{4}$	$\frac{4}{6}$	$\frac{4}{5}$

WRITE THE FRACTION

Write the fraction to tell about the shaded part.

	$\frac{1}{2}$		$\frac{}{4}$
	$\frac{}{4}$		$\frac{}{6}$
	$\frac{}{6}$		$\frac{}{4}$
	$\frac{}{6}$		$\frac{}{6}$
	$\frac{}{6}$		$\frac{}{6}$
	$\frac{}{8}$		$\frac{}{8}$

MEASUREMENTS

HOW LONG?

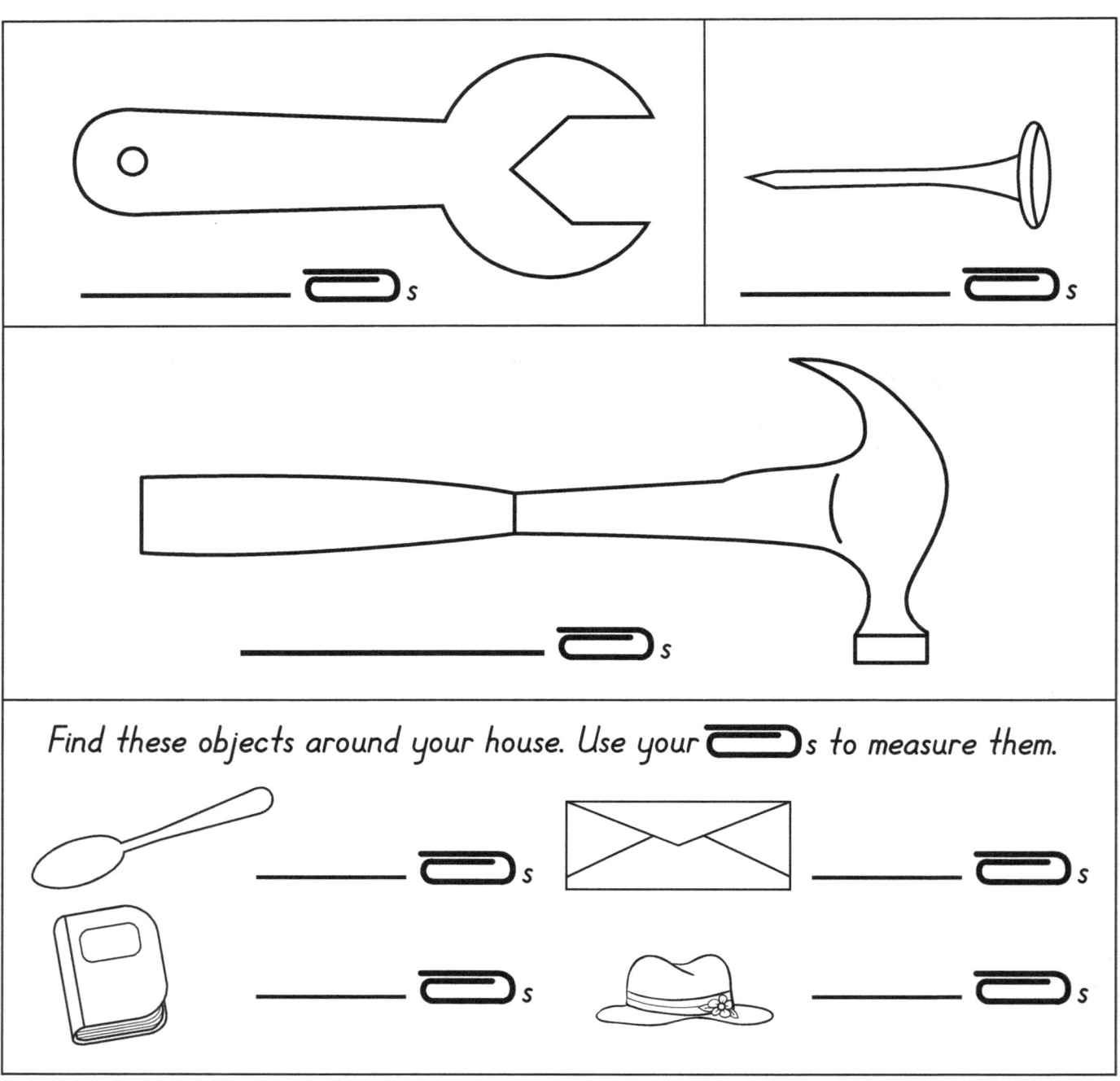

MEASURING INCHES

Color each ruler to the correct inch.

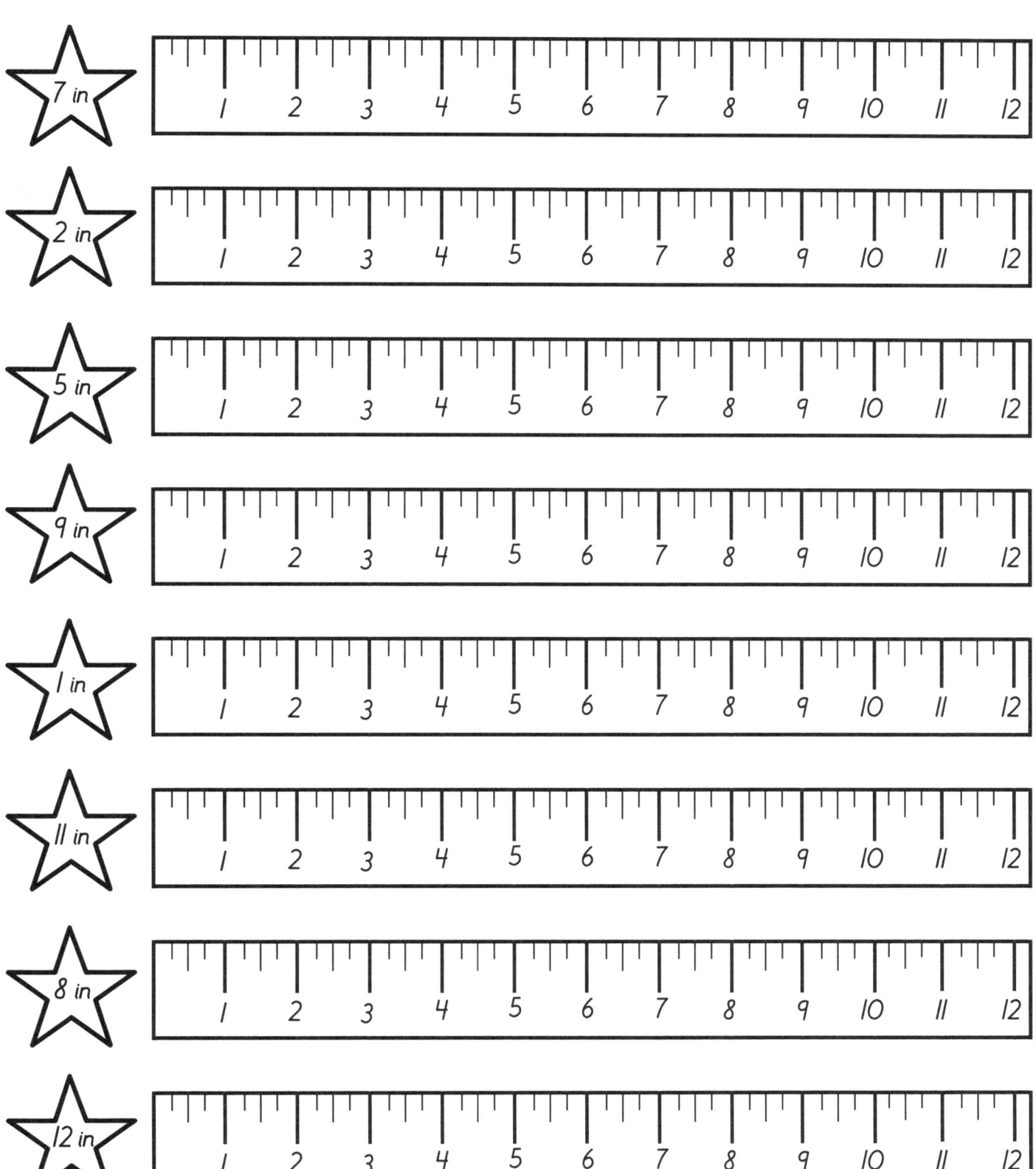

MEASURE THE ROOM

Find the following objects and measure the length using a ruler. Make sure to include the unit (inches or centimeters).

1. Pencil _____

2. Book _____

3. Table _____

4. Fork _____

5. Keyboard _____

6. Sink _____

7. Plate _____

8. Crayon _____

9. Chair _____

10. Hand _____

MEASURING LENGTH

Find each of the below objects around your house. Measure the length using a ruler. Write the measurement in inches AND centimeters.

Item	Inches	Centimeters
(paper clip)	in.	cm.
(pencil)	in.	cm.
(comb)	in.	cm.
(spoon)	in.	cm.
(shoe)	in.	cm.
(key)	in.	cm.

Learning 1st Grade Math Workbook | Autumn McKay

COMPARING HEIGHT

Compare the following animals in terms of height and answer the questions below.

1. Who is the shortest? _____
2. Who is the tallest? _____
3. Tiger is _____ than Mouse.
4. Giraffe is _____ than Hippo.
5. Tiger is _____ than Giraffe.
6. Hippo is _____ than Giraffe.
7. Giraffe is _____ than Mouse.
8. Mouse is _____ than Tiger.
9. Who is taller than Mouse but shorter than Hippo? _____
10. Who is shorter than Giraffe and Shorter than Tiger? _____

HEIGHT MYSTERY

Color the pictures according to the clues in each sentence.

The shortest frog is yellow.
The green frog is taller than the yellow frog, but not the tallest frog.
The tallest frog is orange.

The tallest butterfly is pink.
The purple butterfly is shorter than the pink and red butterfly.
The red butterfly is taller than the purple butterfly.

The tallest tree is green.
The red tree is taller than brown tree.
The brown tree is the shortest tree.

The shortest bird is blue.
The orange bird is taller than the green bird.
The green bird is the tallest bird.

BEACH HEIGHTS

Count how many shells tall each object is and write the answer in the blank.

HOW TALL ARE THE LEAVES?

Draw a line from the top of each leaf over to the ruler to measure the height of each leaf. Write the answer below.

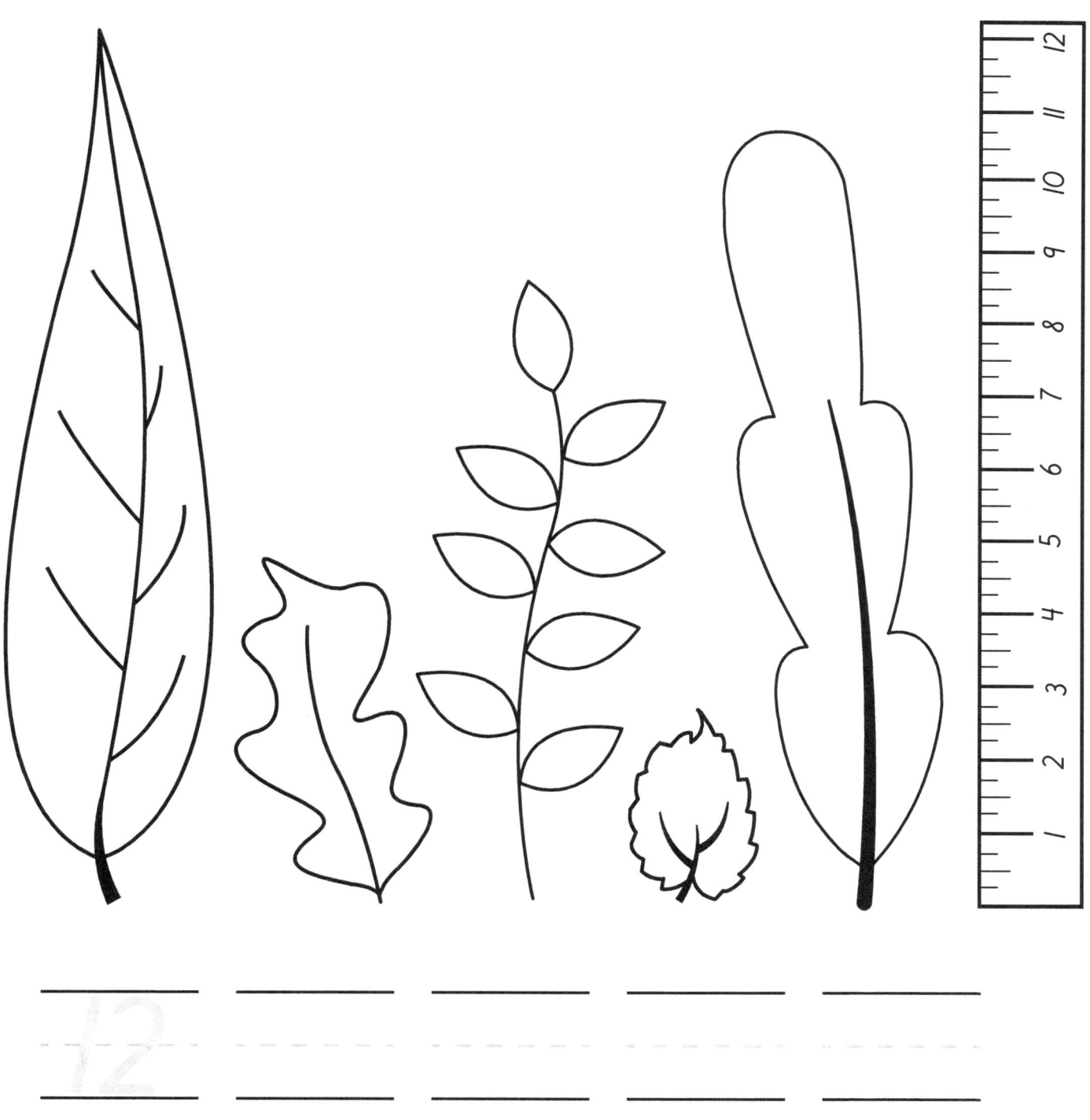

12 ___ ___ ___ ___ ___

WHAT TEMPERATURE IS IT?

Color the thermometer using the color code based on what temperatures you think match.

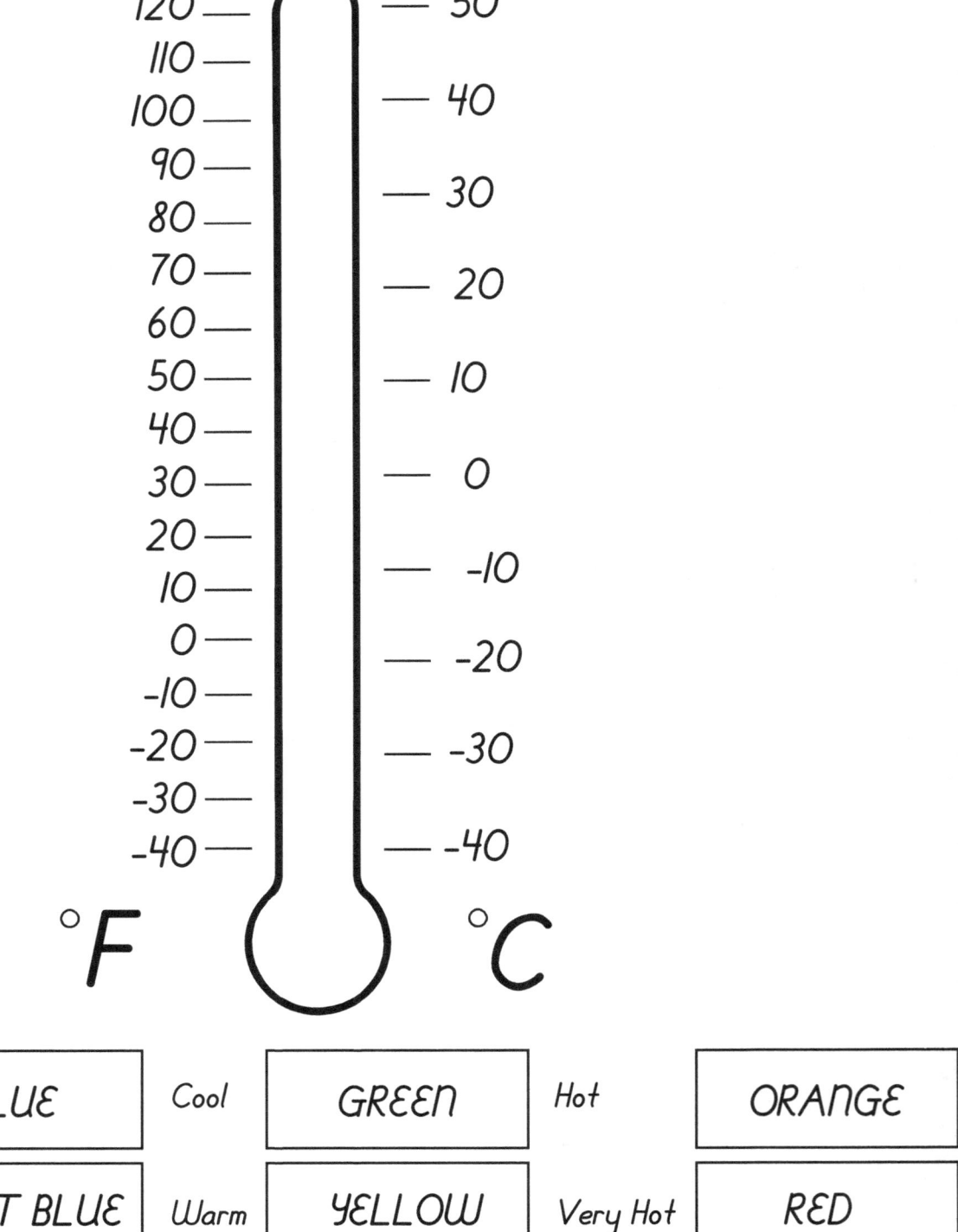

Very cold	BLUE	Cool	GREEN	Hot	ORANGE
Cold	LIGHT BLUE	Warm	YELLOW	Very Hot	RED

READING THERMOMETERS

Use the thermometers to answer the questions.

A	B	C	D	E	F

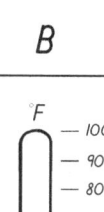
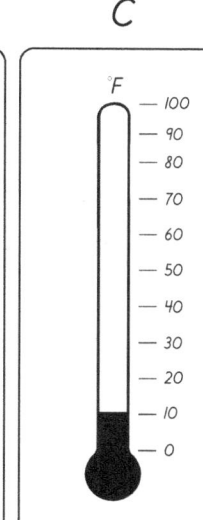
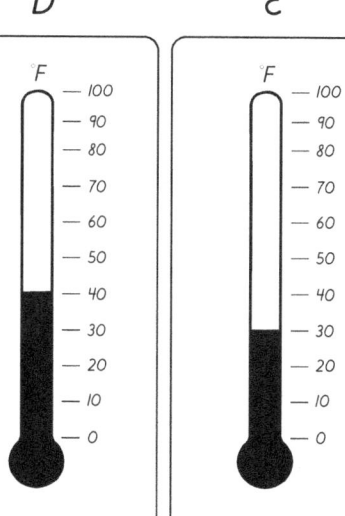
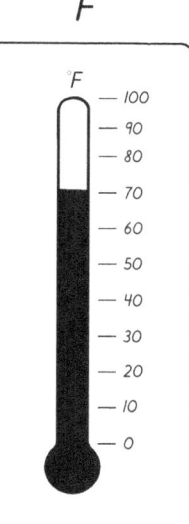

1. Which thermometer has the coldest temperature?

_____

2. Which thermometer has the warmest temperature?

_____

3. Which two thermometers are below freezing?

_____

4. What is the temperature on thermometer D?

_____

5. How much warmer is thermometer F than D?

_____

6. Which thermometer has a temperature of 60°F?

_____

WHAT'S THE TEMPERATURE?

Circle the correct temperature.

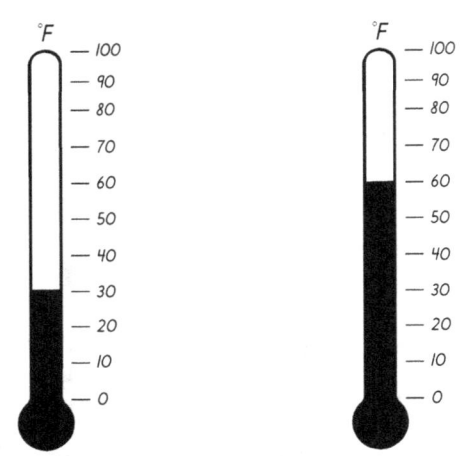

20°   30°

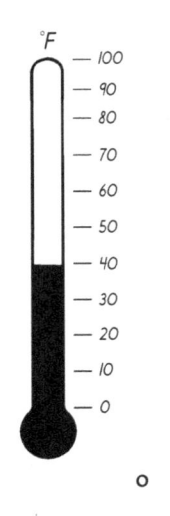

60°   80°

Write the correct temperature.

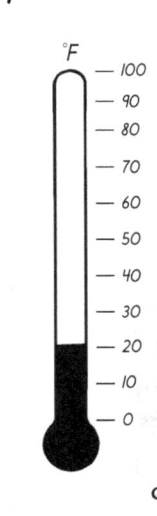

_____ °   _____ °

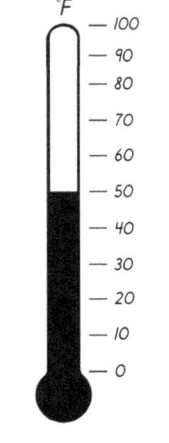

70°   80°

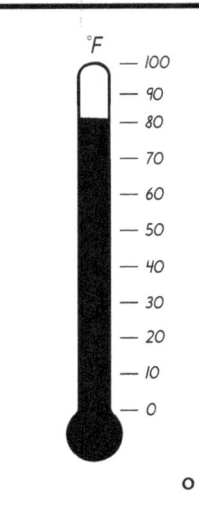

50°   60°

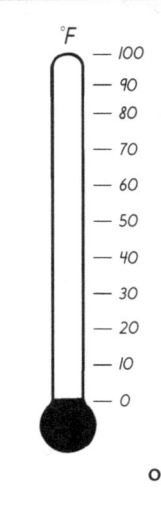

_____ °   _____ °

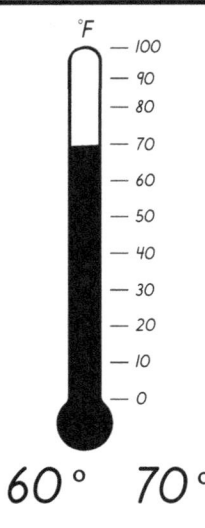

0°   10°

60°   70°

_____ °   _____ °

ILLUSTRATE THE TEMPERATURE

Color in each thermometer to match the temperature given.

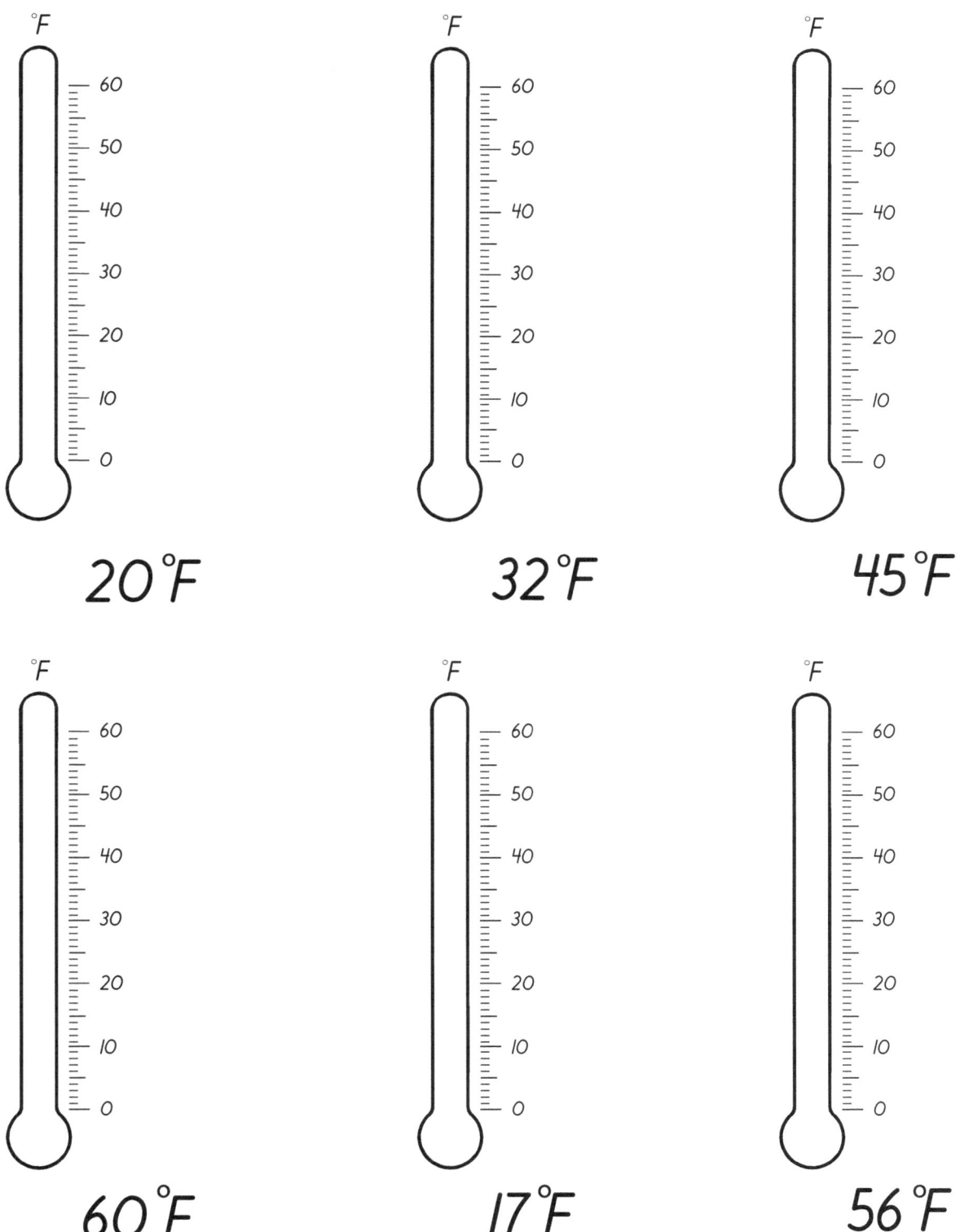

COMPARING WEIGHTS

Look at the two pictures in each box. Color the picture that is heavier.

WHICH IS LIGHTER?

Look at each scale. Determine which object is lighter and color it.

ESTIMATING WEIGHT

Estimate how much each object weighs. Circle the answer that gives the best estimate.

HEAVIER OR LIGHTER?

Look at the below scales and fill in the blanks with "heavier", "lighter", or "the same as".

The pencil case is _____ than the apple.

The pitcher is _____ than the apple.

The tennis ball is _____ the apple.

The feather is _____ than the apple.

The orange is _____ the apple.

The book is _____ than the apple.

WHICH CONTAINER HAS THE LEAST?

Circle the container that has the least amount of liquid.

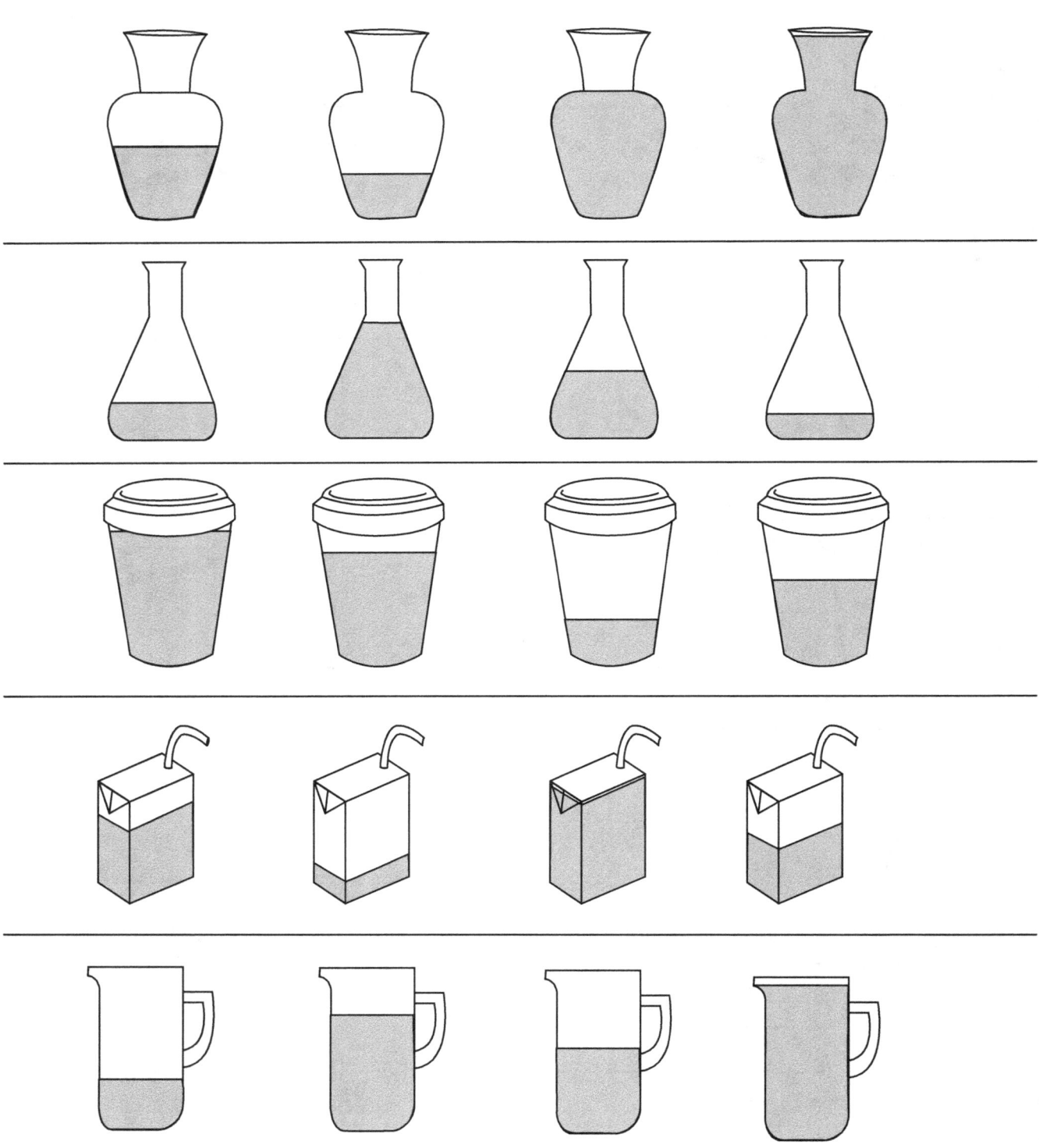

CAPACITY ORDER

Cut out the jars and paste them to the following page from empty to full.

CAPACITY ORDER

CAPACITY

Circle the object that will hold the MOST. Cross out the object that will hold the LEAST. Underline the medium sized object.

HOW MUCH DOES IT HOLD?

less than 1 liter   1 liter   more than 1 liter

Color all the things that hold more than 1 liter red.
Color all the things that hold less than 1 liter yellow.

WORD PROBLEMS

WORD PROBLEM 1

Read each problem carefully two times.
Then solve it in the space below.
Remember to use number models or pictures to help you.

Joseph and Jackie have 20 blocks all together.
Joseph has 5 red blocks and 7 blue blocks.
How many blocks does Jackie have?

Draw it.

Solve it.

WORD PROBLEM 2

Read each problem carefully two times.
Then solve it in the space below.
Remember to use number models or pictures to help you.

Susan collects stickers.
She has 8 large stickers and 12 small stickers.
Susan gave her sister 7 stickers to start her own collection.
How many stickers does Susan have now?

Draw it.

Solve it.

WORD PROBLEM 3

Read each problem carefully two times.
Then solve it in the space below.
Remember to use number models or pictures to help you.

There are many colorful fish swimming in the fish tank.
There are 5 red fish, 7 blue fish, and 6 yellow fish.
How many fish are in the tank?

Draw it.

Solve it.

WORD PROBLEM 4

*Read each problem carefully two times.
Then solve it in the space below.
Remember to use number models or pictures to help you.*

Lisa has 5 nickels. Joey has 2 dimes.
How much money do they have altogether?

Draw it.

Solve it.

WORD PROBLEM 5

Read each problem carefully two times.
Then solve it in the space below.
Remember to use number models or pictures to help you.

Hannah has 1 quarter.
Sam has 3 dimes.
Who has more money?

Draw it.

Solve it.

WORD PROBLEM 6

Read each problem carefully two times.
Then solve it in the space below.
Remember to use number models or pictures to help you.

School starts at 9 o'clock in the morning.
It ends at 3 o'clock in the afternoon.
How many hours is the school day?

Draw it.

Solve it.

WORD PROBLEM 7

Read each problem carefully two times.
Then solve it in the space below.
Remember to use number models or pictures to help you.

The pink crayon is used more than the white crayon.
The white crayon is 3 inches longer than the pink crayon.
If the pink crayon is 1 inch long, how long is the white crayon?

Draw it.

Solve it.

WORD PROBLEM 8

Read each problem carefully two times.
Then solve it in the space below.
Remember to use number models or pictures to help you.

There are 8 cars in the parking lot.
Two cars are parked on the left side and the other cars are parked on the right side.
What fraction of the cars are parked on the right side of the parking lot?

Draw it.

Solve it.

WORD PROBLEM 9

*Read each problem carefully two times.
Then solve it in the space below.
Remember to use number models or pictures to help you.*

There are 14 pieces of fruit in the fruit basket.
There are 4 green apples, 3 red apples, and 4 bananas.
The rest of the fruit is pears.
How many pears are in the fruit basket?

Draw it.

Solve it.

WORD PROBLEM 10

Read each problem carefully two times.
Then solve it in the space below.
Remember to use number models or pictures to help you.

It is Christmas time and Jack and Annie receive a lot of presents.
There are two stacks of presents for Jack and Annie.
There are 15 presents in one stack and 18 presents in the other stack.
How many presents are there altogether?

Draw it.

Solve it.

Congratulations!

You have successfully completed your Learning 1st Grade Math Workbook!

Don't forget to claim your completion certificate. Scan the QR code or visit this link: www.bestmomideas.com/learning-1st-grade-math-certificate

Certificate of Completion

This Certifies That

_____

Has Successfully Trained & Completed the

LEARNING 1ST GRADE MATH WORKBOOK

Parent/Guardian Signature: _____ Date: _____

Thank you for welcoming me in your home! I hope you and your child liked learning together with this book!

If you enjoyed this book, it would mean so much to me if you wrote a review so other moms can learn from your experience.

Autumn@BestMomIdeas.com

Discover Autumn's Other Books

Early Learning Series

Early Learning Workbook Series

  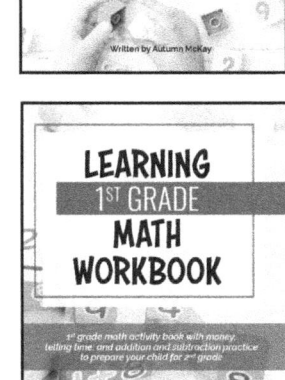

www.BestMomIdeas.com   @BestMomIdeas   Best Mom Ideas

www.ingramcontent.com/pod-product-compliance
Lightning Source LLC
Chambersburg PA
CBHW081752100526
44592CB00015B/2397